ORIGAMI Romantic Hearts

~Lovely Designs for Lovely Moments~

Katrin & Yuri Shumakov

Contents

Introduction.................................... 3	Flying Two-Heart Card ⭐⭐⭐⭐....35
Gallery... 4	Double Heart ⭐⭐⭐................36
Origami Symbols........................... 6	Double Heart Garland ⭐⭐⭐......39
Heart ⭐................................ 7	Double Heart Card ⭐⭐⭐..........40
Clip-Heart ⭐⭐........................... 9	Flying Heart ⭐⭐⭐.................. 41
Clip-Heart Binding ⭐⭐..............12	Valentine ⭐⭐⭐..................... 44
Clip-Heart Bookmark ⭐⭐...........15	Heart Rings 47
Clip-Heart Valentines ⭐⭐.......... 17	-Two-Color Heart Ring ⭐⭐⭐⭐..47
Two-Heart Valentine ⭐⭐...........21	-One-Color Heart Ring ⭐⭐⭐⭐..53
Winged Clip-Heart ⭐⭐⭐............22	Heart Bracelet (2 variants) ⭐⭐⭐⭐.... 54
Heart Card ⭐⭐⭐.......................26	Heart Wristband ⭐⭐⭐⭐.......... 57
Two-Heart Card ⭐⭐⭐⭐............31	Heart Balloon ⭐⭐⭐................ 59
Flying Heart Card ⭐⭐⭐⭐........ 33	About Authors........................ 64

Book Description

ORIGAMI ROMANTIC HEARTS continues the Origami Holiday Series by the Oriland authors and shows how to add lovely origami touch to your romantic moments - whether you celebrate an anniversary, friendship, having a date, wedding time and, of course, Valentine's Day!

Reveal your creativity by taking origami magic into your own hands to make original paper gifts for those whom you love! Do-It-Yourself - fold these lovely original designs by Yuri and Katrin Shumakov. They are a marvelous origami collection that includes 4 various charming hearts, 8 designs of romantic origami cards and valentines, lovely decorative clips for binding, heart bookmarks, garlands and even a heart balloon, as well as fancy origami bijoux like heart rings, heart bracelets and heart wristbands.

There are more than 300 detailed step-by-step colorful diagrams with written instructions and many photos of examples of completed projects that will guide you through folding the 22 original origami designs. For every project, there are recommendations on paper type and size including an indication of the size of the completed model. The designs in this book are from simple to intermediate level of folding and will be great for most origami enthusiasts. They will provide an enjoyable experience for the novice and the expert alike.

Have a creative and fun time with this book making your own Origami Romantic Hearts - lovely designs for lovely moments! Happy hearty folding!

Copyright Notice

ORIGAMI ROMANTIC HEARTS
Lovely Designs for Lovely Moments

Copyright © 2015 by Katrin and Yuri Shumakov. All rights reserved.

No part of this book may be copied or reproduced in any manner whatsoever without written permission from the authors. The designs in this book are intended for personal use only. Any commercial use requires consent from the authors. Contact information may be found at http://www.oriland.com

Origami Designs, Diagrams by Yuri and Katrin Shumakov
Texts, Cover and Interior Design by Katrin and Yuri Shumakov
Photography by Katrin Shumakov

ISBN-13: 978-1507529010
ISBN-10: 1507529015

Printed by CreateSpace, An Amazon.com Company

Introduction

Welcome to the wondrous world of origami where we can turn ordinary flat sheets of paper into beautiful 3-dimensional designs from simple shapes to intricate abstract figures, majestic castles, lovely flowers, little people and the whole variety of objects you can think of! The possibilities of this wonderful art of origami are truly endless - it's like magic!

So, let's bring this origami magic to the holiday time! Continuing our Origami Holiday Series, we are happy to present you with Origami Romantic Hearts - lovely designs for lovely moments!

Whether you celebrate an anniversary, friendship, having a date, wedding time and, of course, Valentine's Day, these designs will bring a lovely origami touch to your romantic time!

The book is offering a hearty collection of our original origami designs. Among them, there are charming one-piece hearts - the Heart, the

V-Day Rendezvous in Oriland's Goblington Kingdom:
Origami Goblin Boy is giving a Clip-Heart Valentine to his Origami Goblin Girl.

Clip-Heart, the Double Heart and the Flying Heart - they all make adorable valentines on their own and also can be used as romantic pins or decorations. The Clip-Heart design is branching into several designs that are easy and fun to make - they are Clip-Heart Valentines, the Two-Heart Valentine and the lovely Heart-Clip Bookmark! The Clip-Heart Binding and the Winged Clip-Heart are perfect to bind your papers in a lovely way.

In this collection, there are also various romantic cards - the Heart Card, the Two-Heart Card, the Flying Heart Card, the Flying Two-Heart Card, the Double Heart Card and Valentines - some are flat, some standing, some cupboard-like and some heart-shaped. There are also the Heart Balloon and the Double Heart Garland that will be wonderful to decorate the space of your romantic event. The Two-Color Heart Ring and the One-Color Heart Ring, the Heart Bracelet in two variations and the elegant Heart Wristband are lovely origami bijoux that are completing this collection of romantic origami designs.

There are more than 300 detailed step-by-step colorful diagrams with written instructions and 100+ photos of examples of completed projects that will guide you through folding the 22 original origami designs. For every project, there are recommendations on paper type and size including an indication of the size of the completed model. The designs in this book are from simple to intermediate level of folding and will be great for most origami enthusiasts. They will provide an enjoyable experience for the novice and the expert alike.

With only paper and folding, you can create lovely origami cards and valentines, charming heart decorations and even heart rings and bracelets! They are both romantic and cute, and so much fun to make as well as a pure delight to present to your dear ones!

Have a creative and fun time with this book making your own Origami Romantic Hearts - lovely designs for lovely moments! Happy hearty folding!

The Authors, Katrin and Yuri Shumakov

Origami Symbols

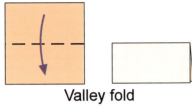
Valley fold

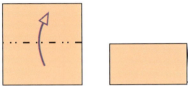
Mountain fold

These simple origami symbols will help you to read diagrams of folding - they show the direction in which the paper has to be folded. Look at the diagram to note which way the lines and arrows - all the symbols demonstrate, and fold your paper according to the diagram. To learn more about origami basics, please visit Oriversity section at our Oriland.com site.

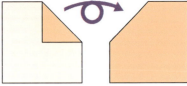
Turn the paper over

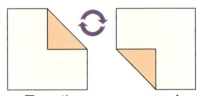
Turn the paper around

Helpful Tips

- Fold the paper on a smooth surface with good lighting.
- Move step by step and don't skip over the next diagram.
- While folding, it's good to pay attention to the diagram of the following step, where the result of the folding is shown.
- After the step is done, don't forget to turn the model into the position shown in the next diagram.
- Smooth out the creases carefully, do not make unnecessary folds.
- If you become confused with the diagrams, don't panic! Study previous steps and see if you missed something. Also, it might be a good idea to start anew.

And most importantly, have fun!

Valley fold and unfold

Mountain fold and unfold

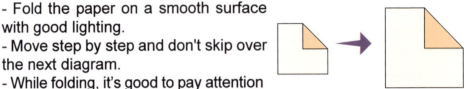
Following diagram is enlarged

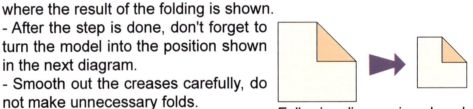
Following diagram is reduced

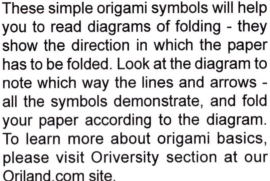
Open and squash

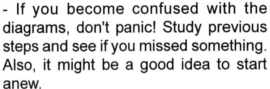
Inside reverse fold

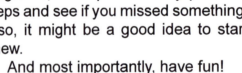
Outside reverse fold

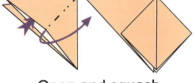
Step fold

Level of folding

★ Simple
★★ Simple-Medium
★★★ Medium
★★★★ Medium-Complex
★★★★★ Complex

The system of levels of folding is more like a guideline and mostly depends of your skills in paper folding. If you are a novice, even the simple level can be challenging for you. And if you are already a connoisseur even a complex model can be simple for you.

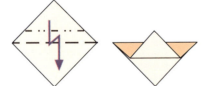
Pull out

Push in. Sink

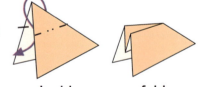
Fold the paper over and over

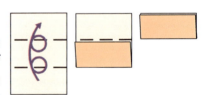
X-ray view ·············

Origami Romantic Hearts

Heart
by Katrin Shumakov

This simple paper heart is fun to fold and give it as a present. This model is also good for making a cute pin or brooch you can wear on Valentine's Day to add a little romantic spirit to your outfit!

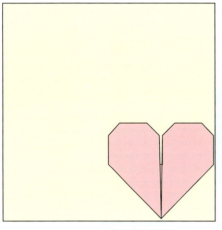

The heart folds from a square. The finished model will be about 1/4 of the size of the original square, as pictured.

Suggested sizes: Use about a 6-inch (15 cm) square to get a 3-inch wide heart.

Suggested paper: From regular origami paper to decorative papers, like chiyogami, foil paper etc. Since the heart displays only one side of paper, it does not matter if you use one-color or duo-color paper.

Suggested color: Any you like, though red and pink shades will work the best.

If using two-color paper, begin with colored side down.

Valley fold the square of paper from left to right. Press the paper flat and unfold it.

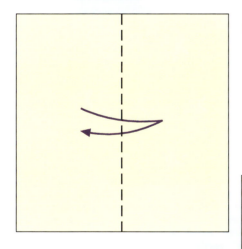

Valley fold the square of paper from top to bottom.

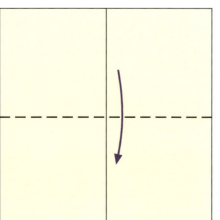

Valley fold the two layers up, so that the raw edges meet the top edge.

Heart © 1996 Katrin Shumakov

Origami Romantic Hearts

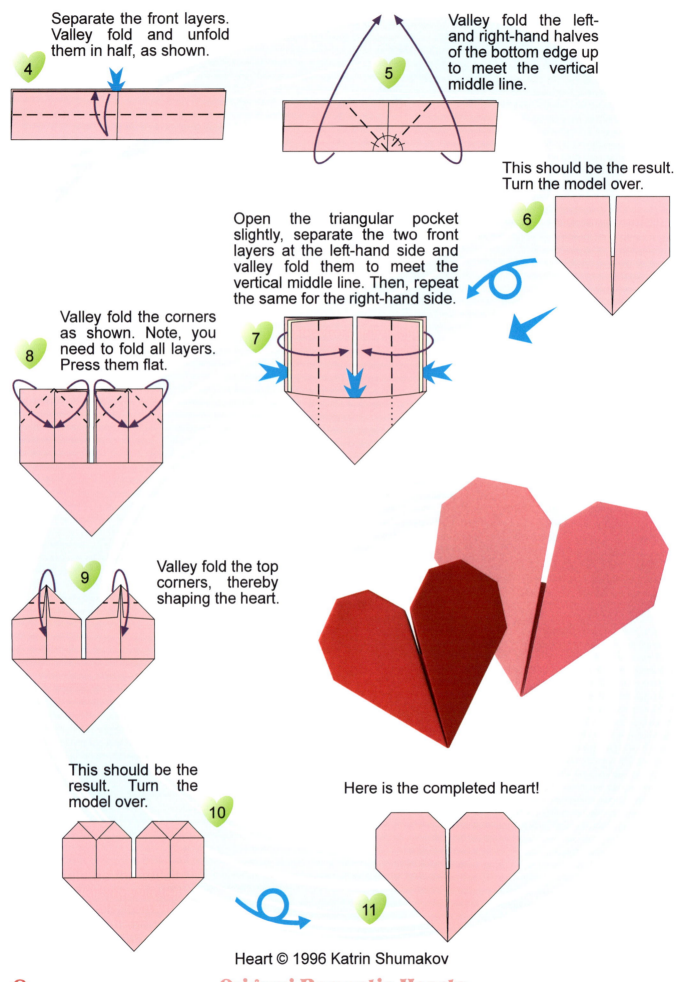

Heart © 1996 Katrin Shumakov

Clip-Heart
by Yuri Shumakov

This heart-shaped clip is easy to fold and fun to play with! Besides being useful as a paper clip, it will be a part of a variety of designs in this book - from simple binding of a few sheets to pretty valentines and even bookmarks.

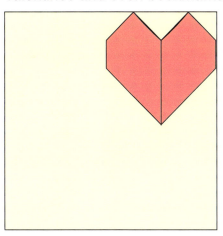

The clip-heart folds from a square. The finished model will be about 1/4 of the size of the original square, as pictured.

Suggested sizes: Use about a 4-inch (10 cm) square to get a 2-inch wide heart.

Suggested paper: From regular origami paper to decorative papers, like chiyogami, foil paper etc. Since the heart displays only one side of paper, it does not matter if you use one-color or duo-color paper.

Suggested color: Any you like.

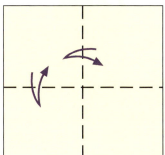

1 *If using two-color paper, begin with colored side down.*

Valley fold the opposite sides together in both directions, and open them up.

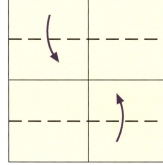

2 Valley fold the top and bottom sides over to meet the horizontal middle fold-line.

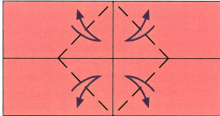

4 Valley fold both halves of the top edge over to meet the vertical middle fold-line. Press the folds until horizontal middle fold-line and unfold them. Repeat with the bottom edge.

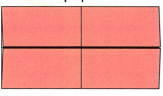

3 This should be the result. Turn the paper over.

Clip-Heart © 2006 Yuri Shumakov

Origami Romantic Hearts

Shape the paper along the 'valley' fold-lines, at the same time, mountain fold the middle, as shown.

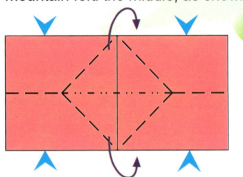

Continue bringing the middle points down, thereby shaping the model as shown in the next step.

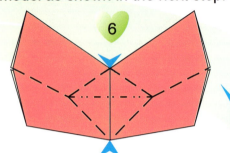

This should be the result. Working with the right-hand half, open out the front layer slightly.

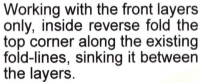

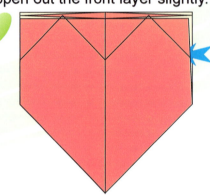

Valley fold and unfold the corners at the top, as shown. Repeat behind.

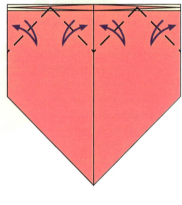

Working with the front layers only, inside reverse fold the top corner along the existing fold-lines, sinking it between the layers.

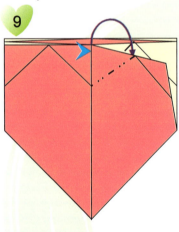

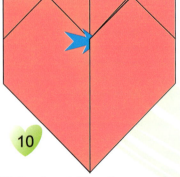

This should be the result. Continue working with the right-hand half, from the middle, open out the front layer slightly as shown.

Inside reverse fold the top right-hand corner (all its layers) along the existing fold-lines, sinking it inside the model.

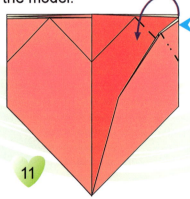

Insert the corner into the pocket, as shown, thereby locking the right-hand half of the model.

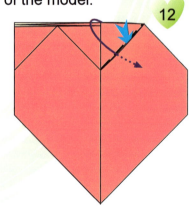

Clip-Heart © 2006 Yuri Shumakov

10 Origami Romantic Hearts

This should be the result. Working with the left-hand half, open out the front layer slightly.

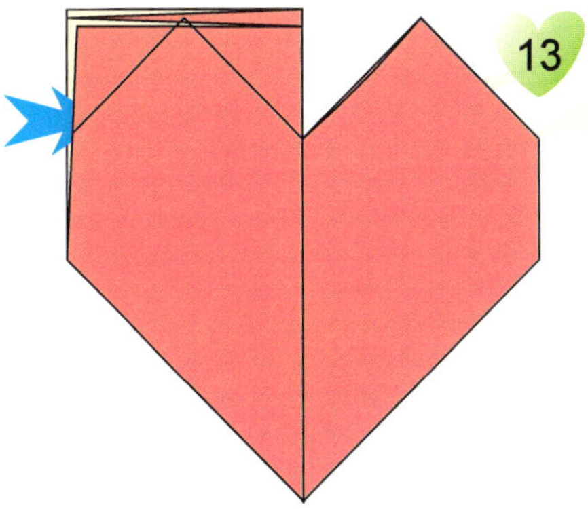

13

14 Working with the front layers only, inside reverse fold the top corner along the existing fold-lines, sinking it between the layers.

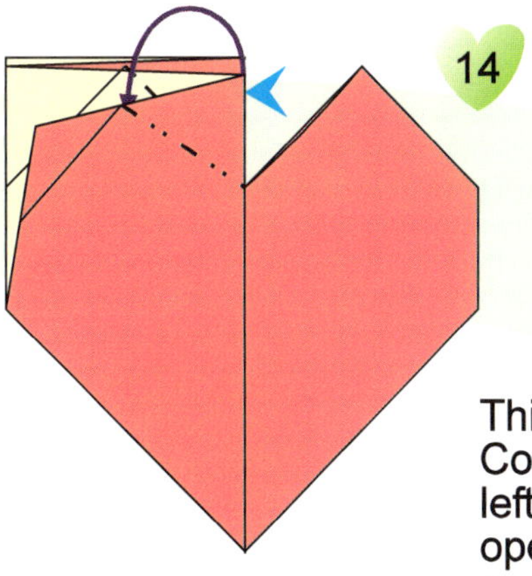

This should be the result. Continue working with the left-hand half, from the middle, open out the front layer slightly as shown.

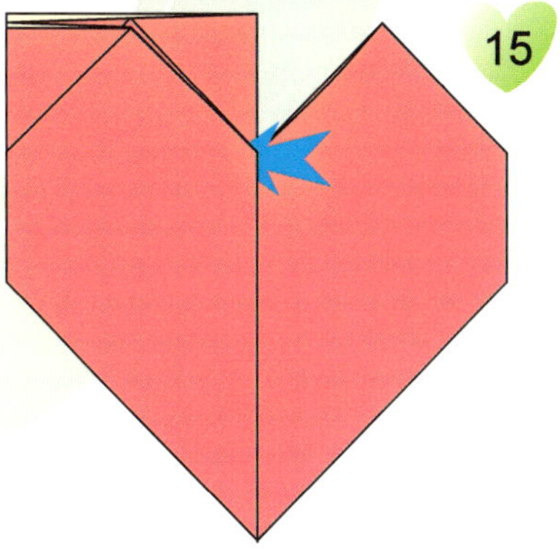

15

Inside reverse fold the top left-hand corner (all its layers) along the existing fold-lines, sinking it inside the model.

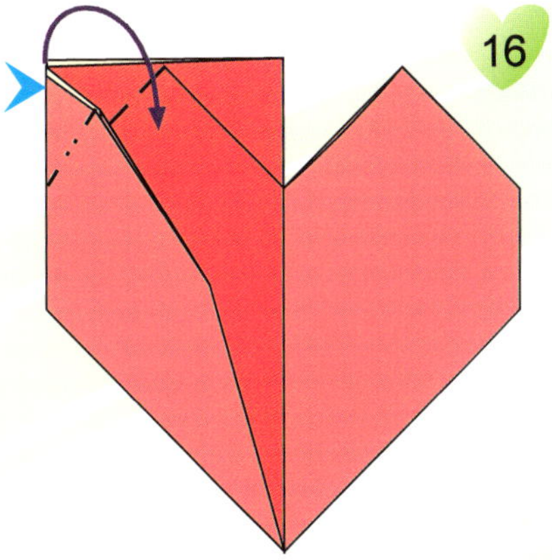

16

Insert the corner into the pocket, as shown, thereby locking the left-hand half of the model.

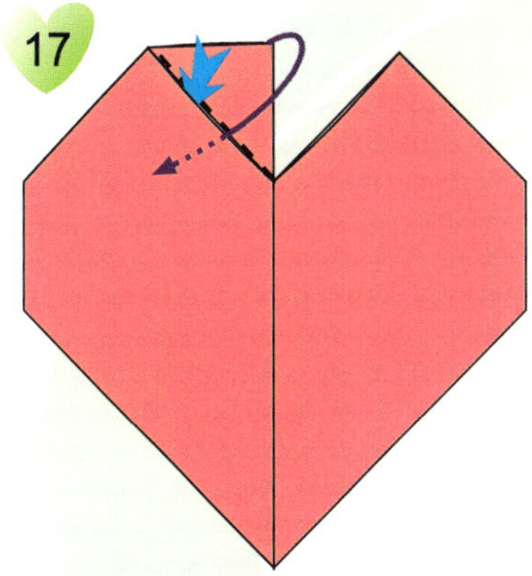

17

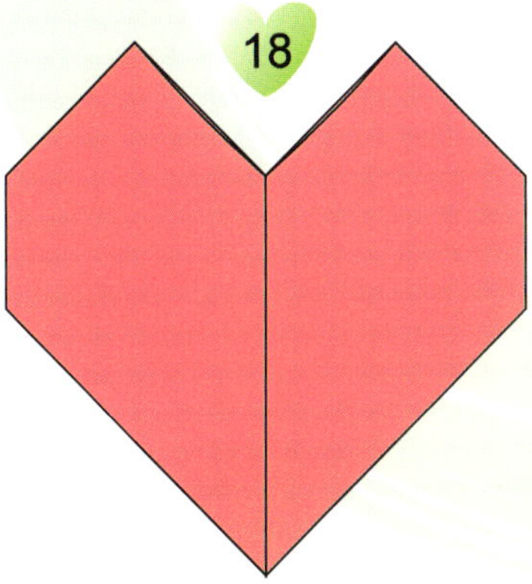

18

The clip-heart is ready.

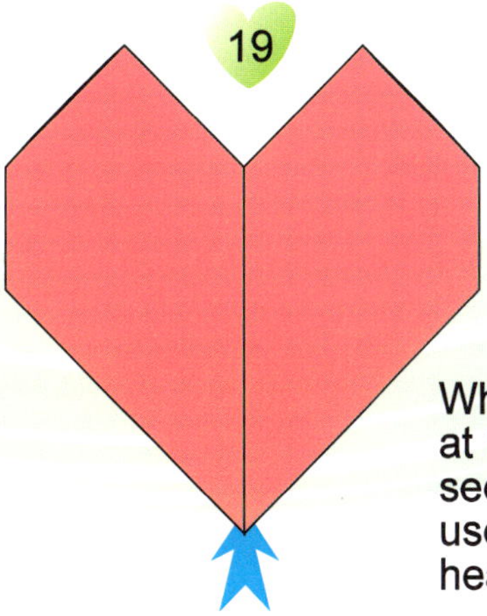

19

When separating the layers at the bottom slightly, you'll see a slit, which will be used in order to attach the heart to something...

Clip-Heart © 2006 Yuri Shumakov

Clip-Heart Binding
by Yuri Shumakov

This clip-heart is perfect to bind a few sheets together and add a romantic touch to your paperwork! For a very special message, you can layer two nice paper squares of different sizes and bind them in a heartily way.

Suggested sizes: For the clip-heart, use about a 4-inch (10 cm) square to get a 2-inch wide heart.

Take a few sheets of paper to bind them with this clip-heart.

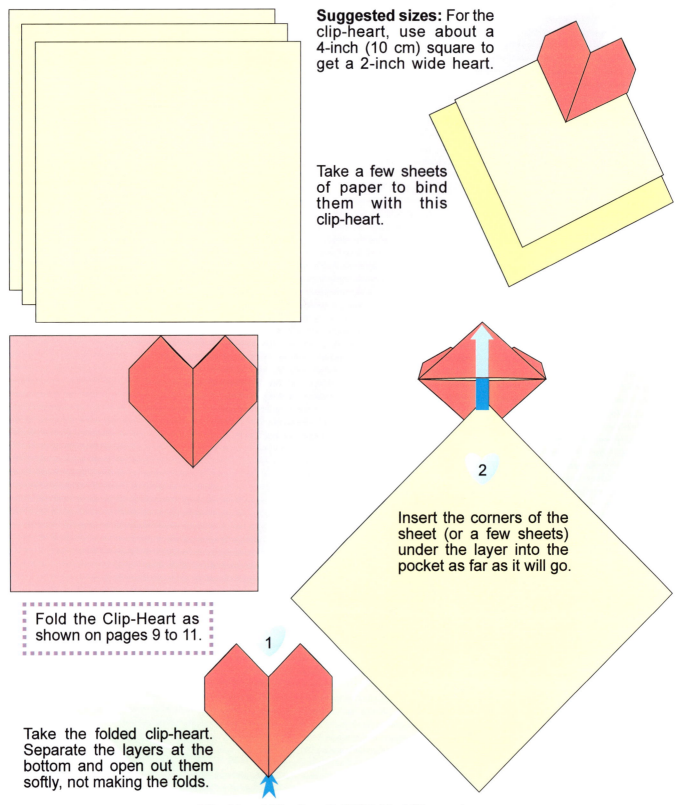

Fold the Clip-Heart as shown on pages 9 to 11.

Take the folded clip-heart. Separate the layers at the bottom and open out them softly, not making the folds.

Insert the corners of the sheet (or a few sheets) under the layer into the pocket as far as it will go.

Clip-Heart Binding © 2006 Yuri Shumakov

Valley fold the layers down, thereby locking the corners of the sheets by the paper clip.

Mountain fold the heart in half as shown, just to strengthen the paper lock, and then release it.

Here is the completed clip-heart binding.

You can bind two nice squares of different sizes for a very special message!

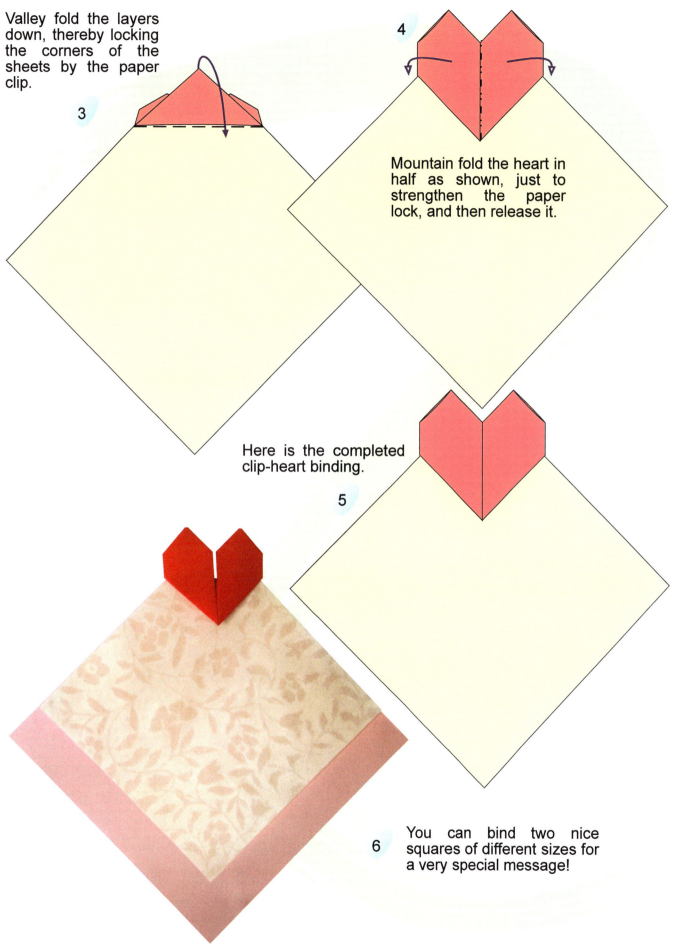

Clip-Heart Binding © 2006 Yuri Shumakov

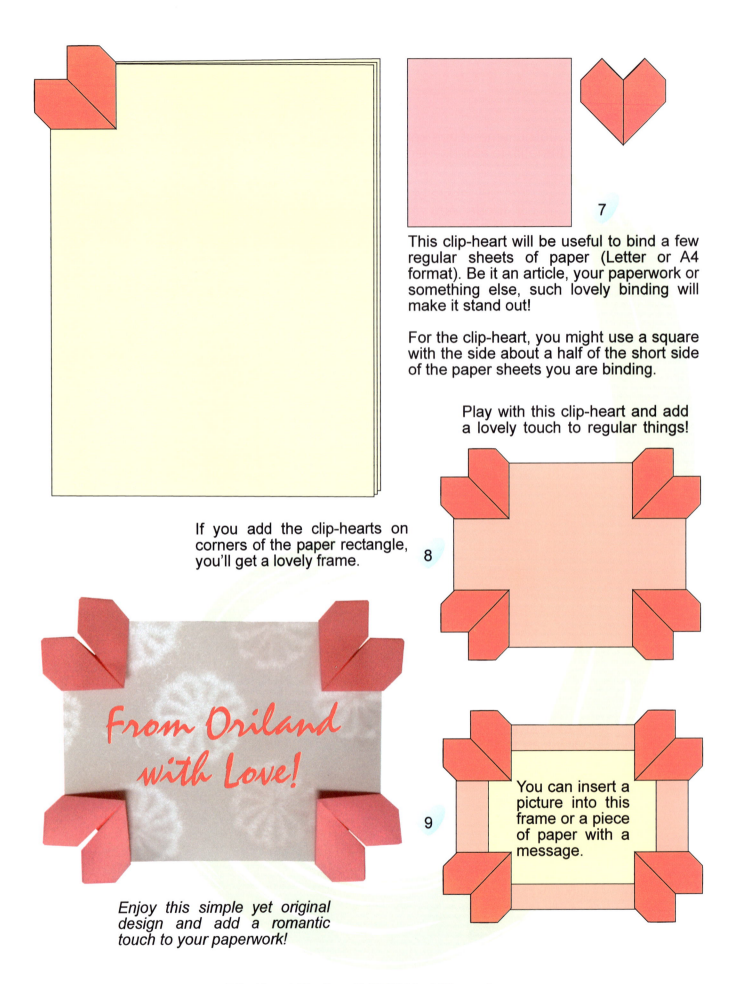

7

This clip-heart will be useful to bind a few regular sheets of paper (Letter or A4 format). Be it an article, your paperwork or something else, such lovely binding will make it stand out!

For the clip-heart, you might use a square with the side about a half of the short side of the paper sheets you are binding.

Play with this clip-heart and add a lovely touch to regular things!

If you add the clip-hearts on corners of the paper rectangle, you'll get a lovely frame.

8

9

You can insert a picture into this frame or a piece of paper with a message.

From Oriland with Love!

Enjoy this simple yet original design and add a romantic touch to your paperwork!

Clip-Heart Binding © 2006 Yuri Shumakov

Clip-Heart Bookmark
by Yuri and Katrin Shumakov

It's super easy to make a lovely bookmark with the clip-heart and a strip of paper. Such a bookmark can make a wonderful present to a book lover!

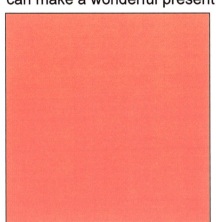

Suggested sizes: Use about a 4-inch (10 cm) square to get a 2-inch wide heart. For the bookmark itself, take a strip of paper, about 8 inches long or so. You may use thick paper of the needed size, say 1 x 8 inches, just to attach it to the clip-heart. Alternatively, you can use the regular paper a bit wider, say 2 x 8 inches or so, to fold it into a stalk and then attach it to the clip-heart.

Suggested paper: For the clip-heart, a variety of papers can be used from regular origami paper to decorative papers, like chiyogami, foil paper etc. For the bookmark itself, you may use thick paper like lightweight cardstock, as well as more thin paper like regular copy paper etc.

Fold the Clip-Heart as shown on pages 9 to 11.

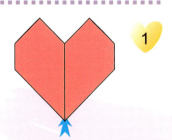

1

Take the folded clip-heart. Separate the layers at the bottom and open out them softly, not making the folds.

2

When working with the strip of thick paper of the needed size, insert the end of the paper strip into the pocket of the heart as far as it will go.

3

Valley fold the layers down, thereby locking the bookmark by the paper clip.

4

Mountain fold the heart in half as shown, just to strengthen the paper lock, and then release it.

5

Here is the Clip-Heart Bookmark.

Clip-Heart Bookmark © 2006 Yuri and Katrin Shumakov

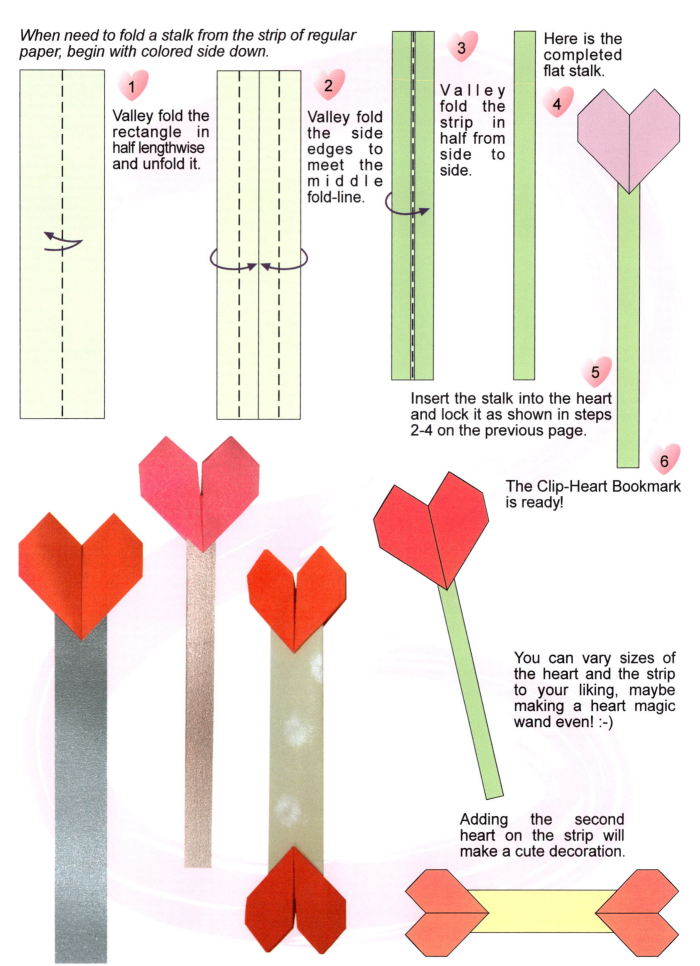

When need to fold a stalk from the strip of regular paper, begin with colored side down.

1. Valley fold the rectangle in half lengthwise and unfold it.
2. Valley fold the side edges to meet the middle fold-line.
3. Valley fold the strip in half from side to side.
4. Here is the completed flat stalk.
5. Insert the stalk into the heart and lock it as shown in steps 2-4 on the previous page.
6. The Clip-Heart Bookmark is ready!

You can vary sizes of the heart and the strip to your liking, maybe making a heart magic wand even! :-)

Adding the second heart on the strip will make a cute decoration.

Clip-Heart Bookmark © 2006 Yuri and Katrin Shumakov

Clip-Heart Valentines
by Yuri and Katrin Shumakov

You can make very pretty Valentine's Day cards with the clip-hearts. They are easy and fun to fold and a pleasure to present them to your special friends!

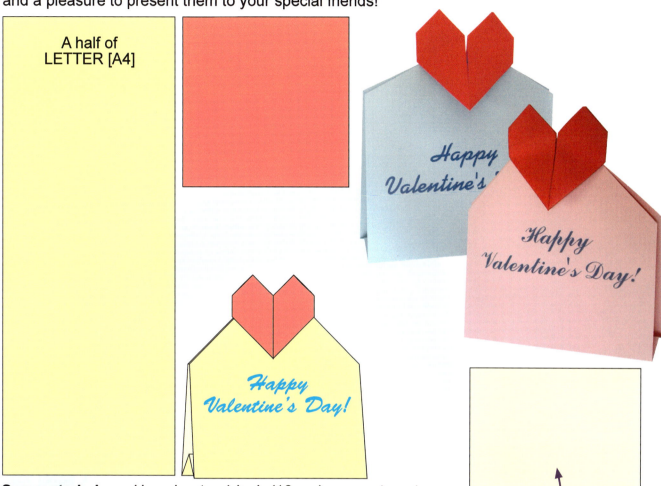

Suggested sizes: Use about a 4-inch (10 cm) square to get a 2-inch wide heart.
For the card, take a half of the regular sheet of Letter or A4 format. It can be a 1:3 rectangle, 4x12 inches (10x30 cm) in size or about.

The size of the resulted card will be a bit less than a half of the original rectangle, as pictured.

Suggested paper: For the clip-heart, a variety of papers can be used from regular origami paper to decorative papers, like chiyogami, foil paper etc. For the card itself, you may use regular copy paper, decorative papers, lightweight cardstock etc.

Suggested color: Any you like.

1. Fold the Clip-Heart as shown on pages 9 to 11.

If using two-color paper, begin with colored side down.

2. Place the rectangle in portrait position. Fold it in half from bottom to top.

Clip-Heart Valentines © 2006 Yuri and Katrin Shumakov

Origami Romantic Hearts

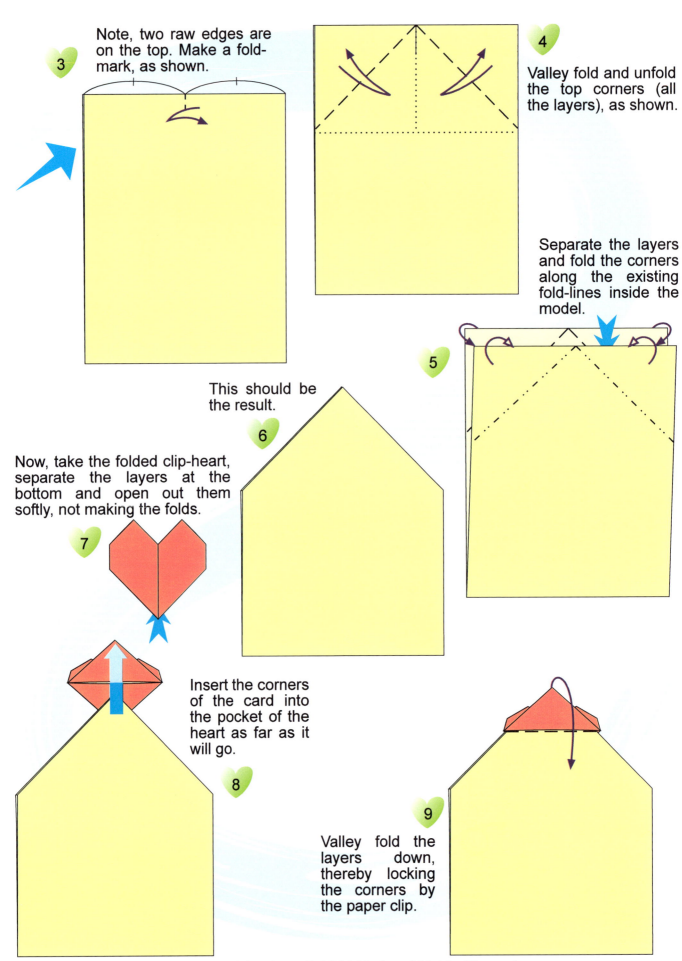

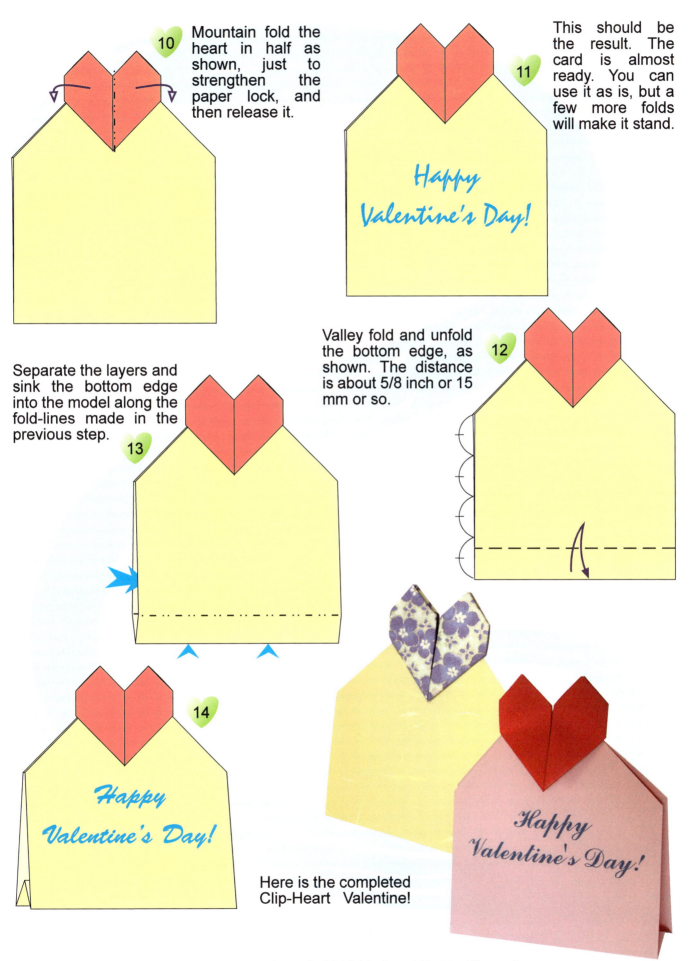

Card Variation

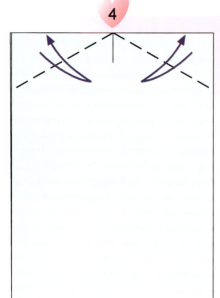

If in step 4, you fold the top corners in this way…

You will get a nice variation of the Clip-Heart Valentine.

Don't forget that you can use fancy paper for the card to make it stand out.

Enjoy making these attractive Clip-Heart Valentines, varying sizes, paper and colors, and gladden your friends with them!

Clip-Heart Valentines © 2006 Yuri and Katrin Shumakov

Two-Heart Valentine
by Yuri and Katrin Shumakov

This is a double lovely variation of Clip-Heart Valentine that features two hearts. Just make alternative final steps and voila!

Make the first 11 steps of the Clip-Heart Valentine in the same way as shown on pages 17 to 19.

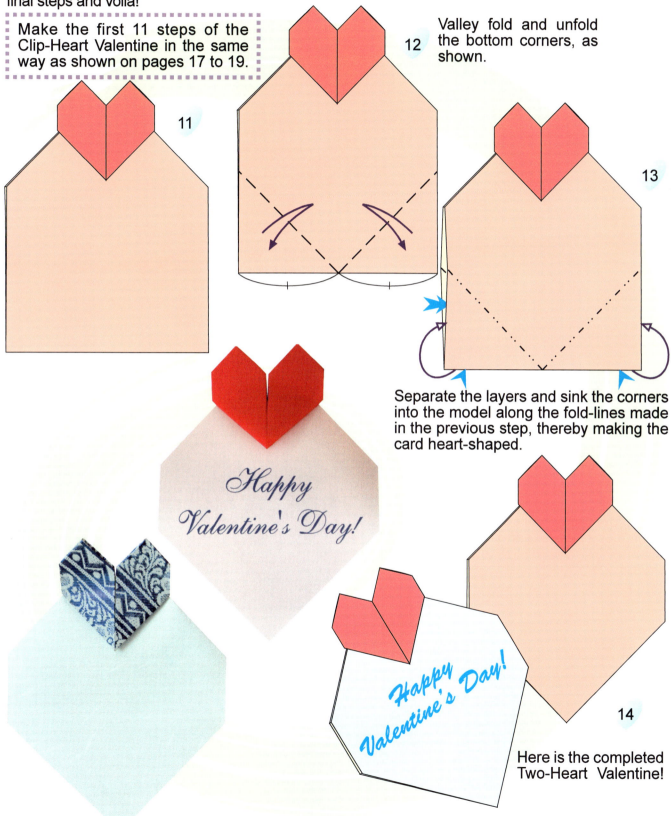

12. Valley fold and unfold the bottom corners, as shown.

13. Separate the layers and sink the corners into the model along the fold-lines made in the previous step, thereby making the card heart-shaped.

14. Here is the completed Two-Heart Valentine!

Two-Heart Valentine © 2006 Yuri and Katrin Shumakov

Winged Clip-Heart
by Yuri Shumakov

This is a clever origami clip in a shape of a winged heart, which can hold several sheets of paper together. When folded from foil paper - it can hold up to 12 sheets of regular copy paper. Let your papers be bound creatively!

The clip folds from a square. The finished model will be inscribed into 1/4 of the size of the original square, as pictured.

The long side of the clip (the wing's span) will be a half of the diagonal of the original square; the height of the clip's heart will be 1/4 of this diagonal.

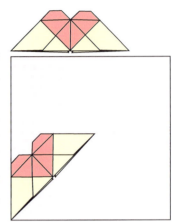

Suggested sizes: Use about a 4-inch (10 cm) square to get a 2-3/4-inch (7 cm) wide clip. This size will work great with regular sheets of Letter or A4 formats.

Suggested paper: It's preferably to use origami foil paper. This way, the folds will be held more securely and the heart can be embossed. Since the clip displays two sides of paper, it is better to use duo-color paper.

Suggested color: Any you like. The brighter heart will be, the better.

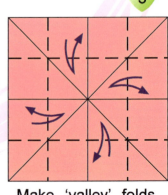

If using two-color paper, begin with colored side down.

1 Valley fold the opposite sides together in both directions, and open them up.

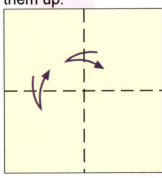

2 Valley fold the opposite corners together, in turn, to mark the diagonal fold lines, and open them up. Then, turn the paper over.

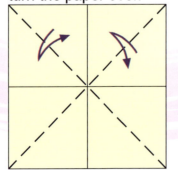

3 Make 'valley' folds, as shown.

Winged Clip-Heart © 2006 Yuri Shumakov

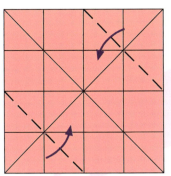

 4

Valley fold two opposite corners over to meet the middle point.

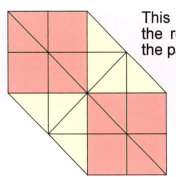

This should be the result. Turn the paper over.

 5

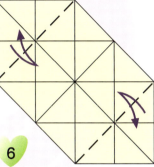

Valley fold and unfold the opposite corners as shown. Then, turn the paper over.

Along the existing fold-lines, valley fold the side points into the middle, thereby making two small squares. Squash them flat.

 7

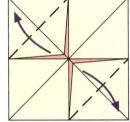

8

Valley fold the front layer of each of two small squares as shown.

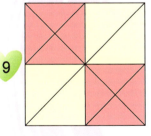

9

This should be the result. Turn the paper over.

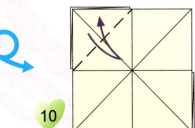

10

Valley fold all the layers of the upper left-hand corner. Press it flat and unfold it.

Valley fold all the layers of the opposite corner.

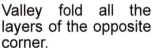

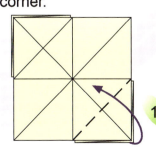

11

12

Valley fold the flap as shown.

Winged Clip-Heart © 2006 Yuri Shumakov

Origami Romantic Hearts 23

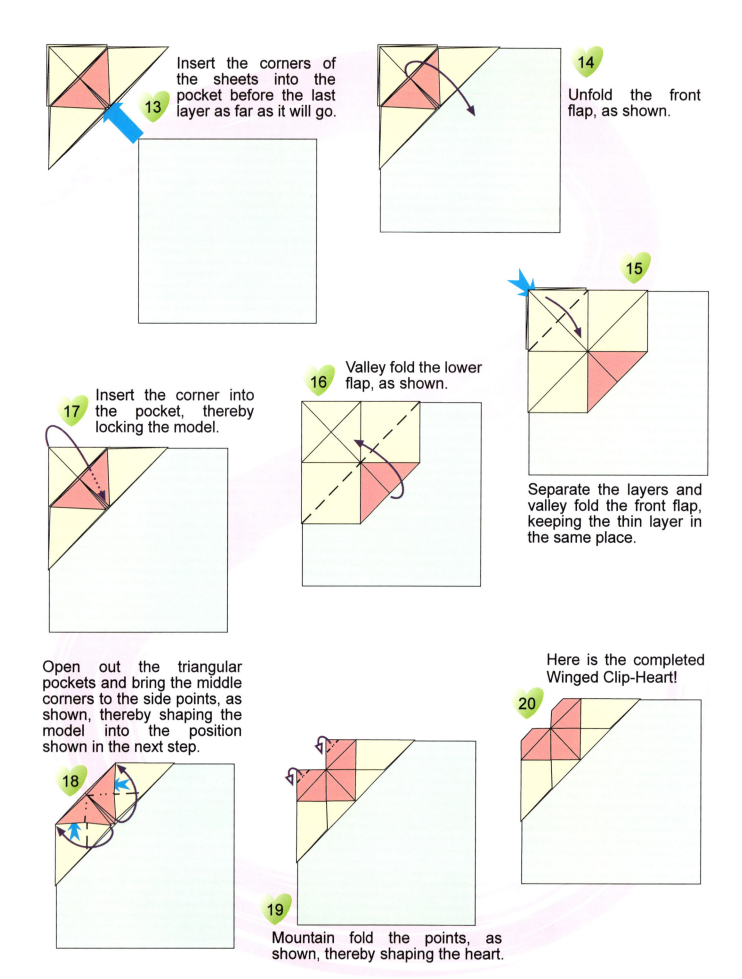

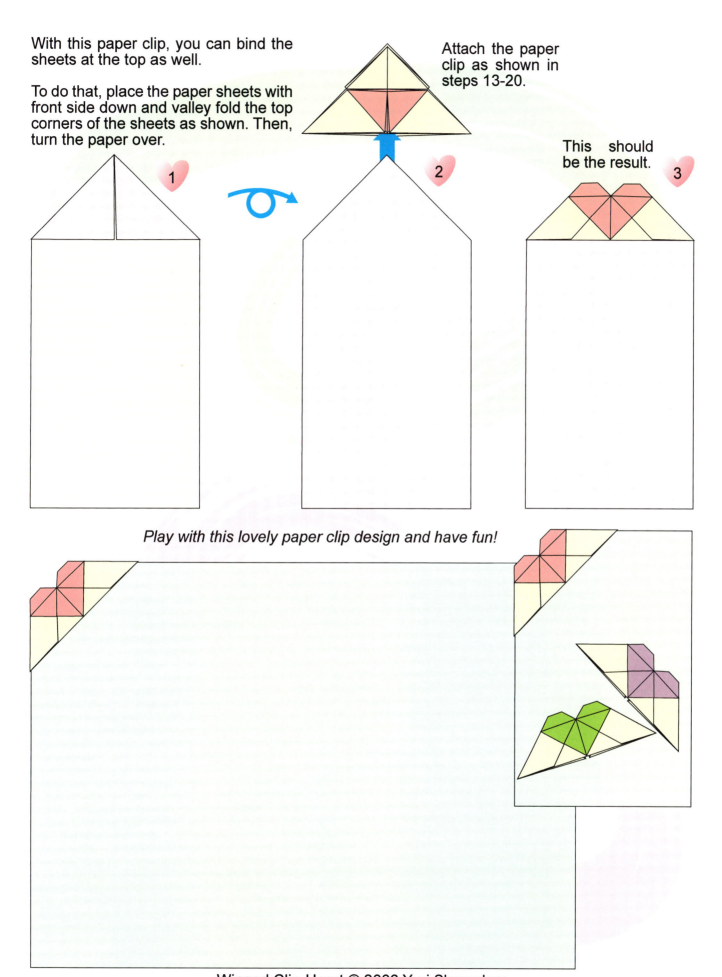

Heart Card
by Katrin and Yuri Shumakov

This is a lovely card design that folds from a square and features a heart on its top edge. It is fun to fold and will be perfect for any romantic occasion!

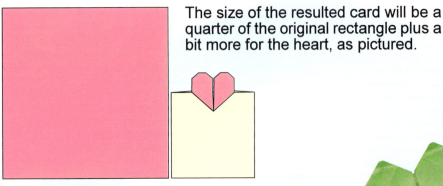

The size of the resulted card will be a quarter of the original rectangle plus a bit more for the heart, as pictured.

Suggested sizes: Use a large square for practice. When mastered the model, use about a 6-inch (15 cm) square to get a cute card, 3x3-1/2-inch (7.5x9 cm) in size.

Suggested paper: From regular origami paper to decorative papers, like chiyogami, foil paper etc. Since the card displays two sides of paper, it is better to use duo-color paper.

Suggested color: Any you like. The brighter contrast between two sides of paper will be, the better.

If using two-color paper, begin with that side up, which color you would like to have on the heart.

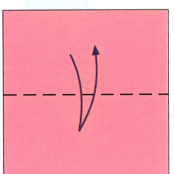

1 Valley fold the square in half from top to bottom and unfold it.

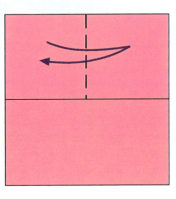

2 Valley fold the square in half from left to right. Do not press the paper completely flat, but press down on it at the top half of the paper. Then, unfold it.

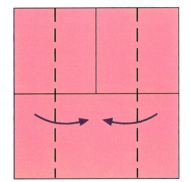

3 Valley fold the left- and right-hand edges over to meet the vertical middle fold-line.

Heart Card © 1996 Katrin and Yuri Shumakov

Origami Romantic Hearts

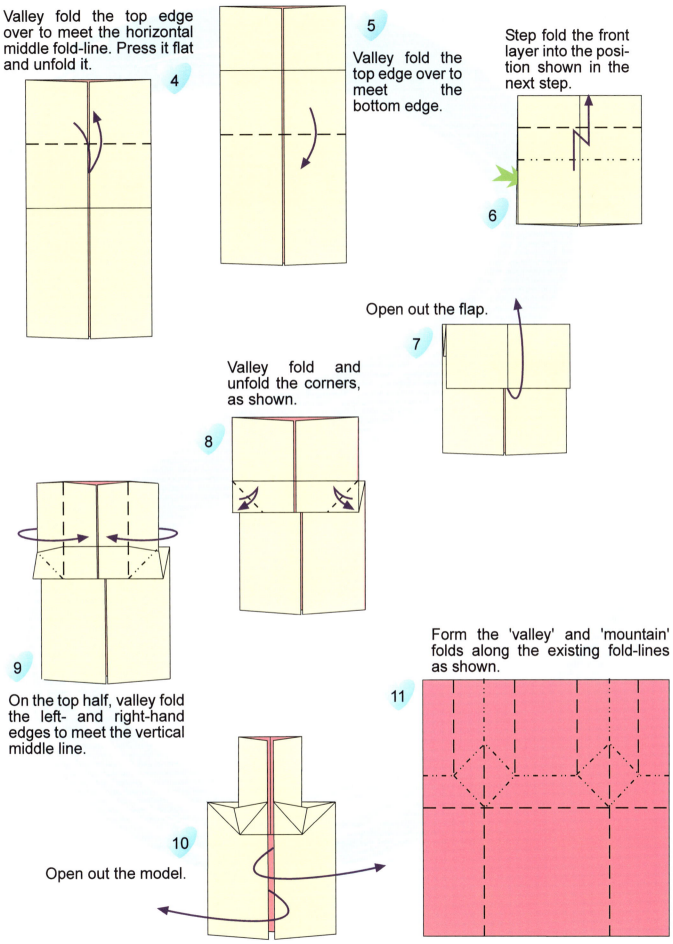

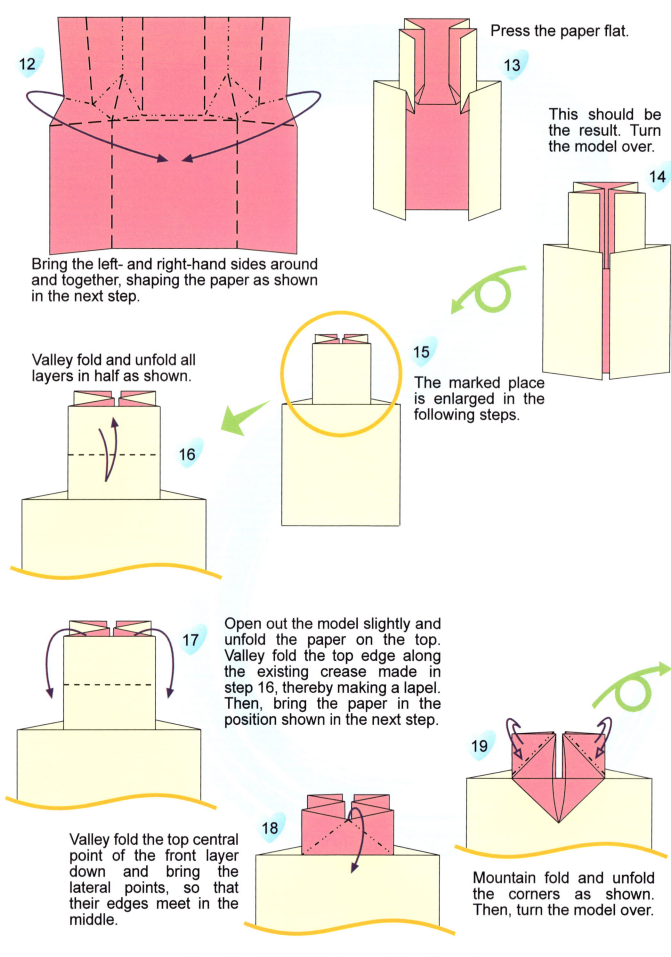

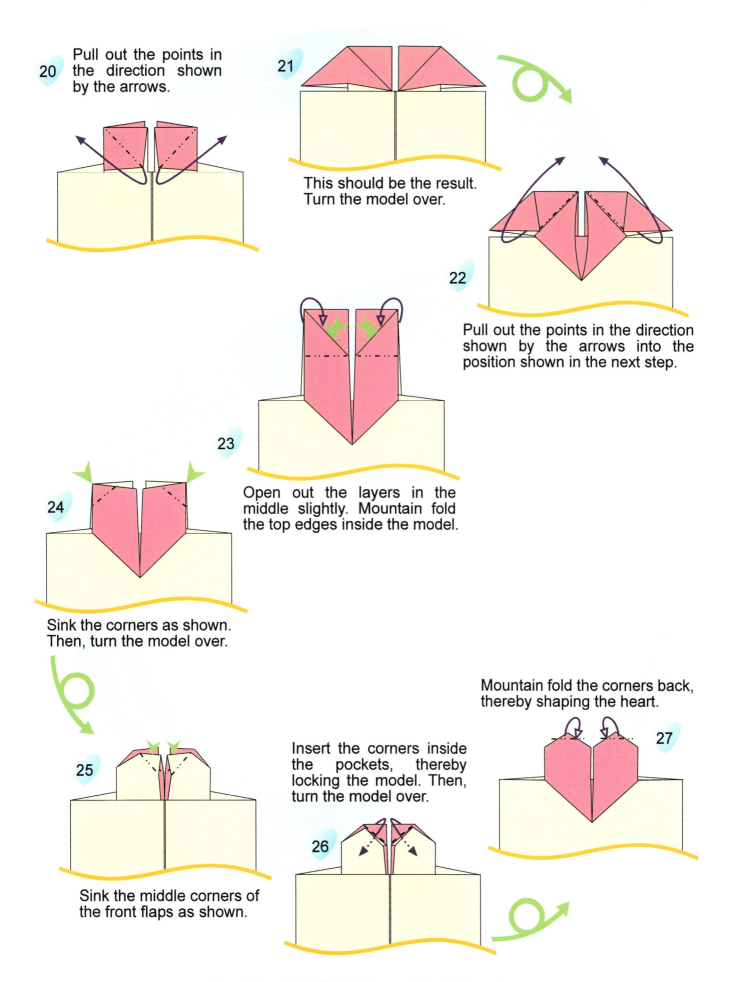

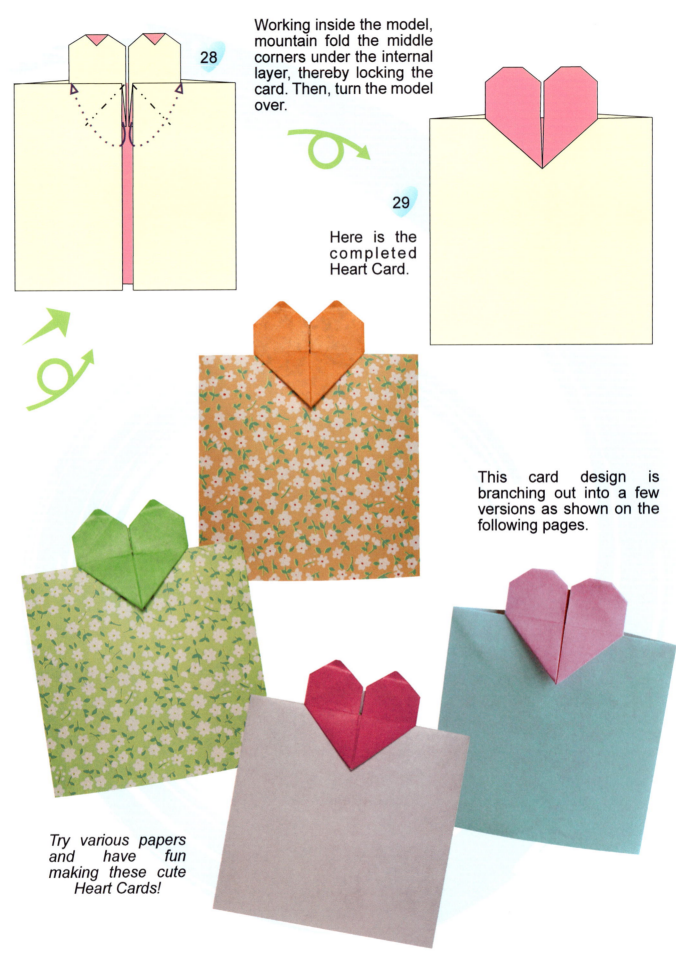

28

Working inside the model, mountain fold the middle corners under the internal layer, thereby locking the card. Then, turn the model over.

29

Here is the completed Heart Card.

This card design is branching out into a few versions as shown on the following pages.

Try various papers and have fun making these cute Heart Cards!

Heart Card © 1996 Katrin and Yuri Shumakov

Two-Heart Card
by Katrin and Yuri Shumakov

This twice as lovely card is based on the previous card design and also folds from a square. It features two hearts - one is the body of the card itself and the other one is on its top edge. This card is both romantic and cute!

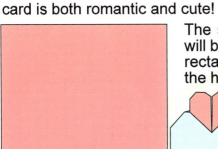

The size of the resulted card will be a quarter of the original rectangle plus a bit more for the heart, as pictured.

Suggested sizes: Use a large square for practice. When mastered the model, use about a 6-inch (15 cm) square to get a card, 3x3-1/2-inch (7.5x9 cm) in size.

Suggested paper: From regular origami paper to decorative papers, like chiyogami, foil paper etc. Since the card displays two sides of paper, it is better to use duo-color paper.

Suggested color: Any you like. The brighter contrast between two sides of paper will be, the better.

If using two-color paper, begin with that side up, which color you would like to have on the heart.

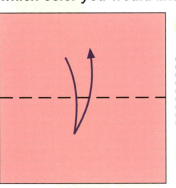

1

Fold first 27 steps along the diagrams of the Heart Card, pages 26 to 29.

Valley fold the square in half from top to bottom and unfold it.

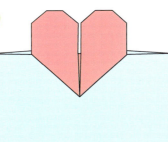

27

There should be the result. Turn the model over.

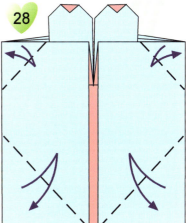

28

Valley fold the corners of the card as shown, so that they loosely shape a heart. Press the folds flat and unfold them.

Two-Heart Card © 1996 Katrin and Yuri Shumakov

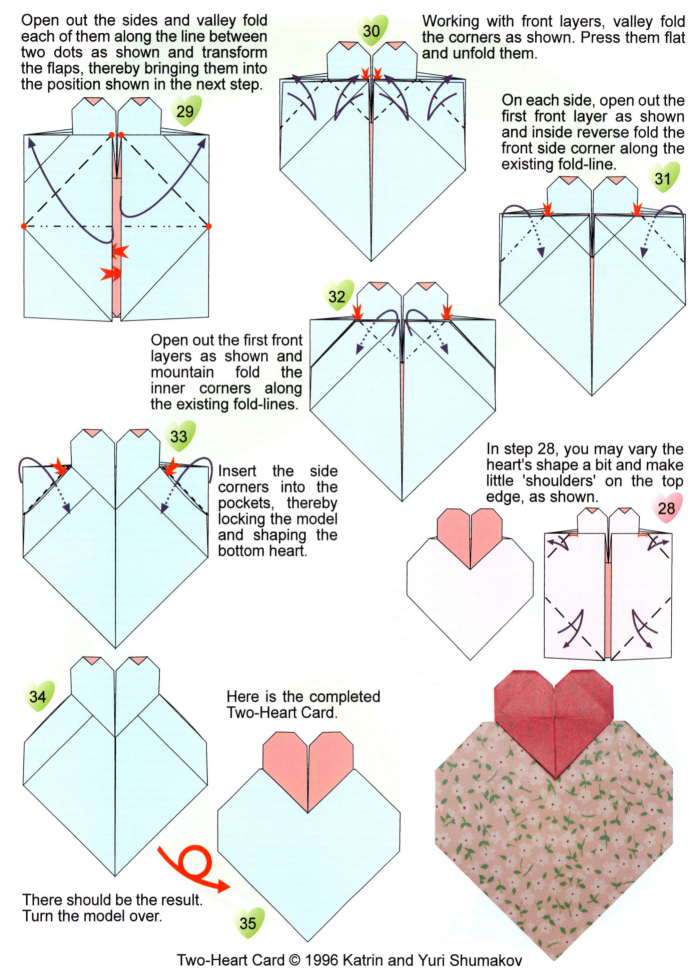

Flying Heart Card
by Katrin and Yuri Shumakov

This design is based on the Heart Card and features an adorable heart with wings that can be plain or pleated. This card is fun to make and a delight to present to a dear friend!

The size of the resulted card will be a quarter of the original rectangle plus a bit more for the heart, as pictured.

Suggested sizes: Use a large square for practice. When mastered the model, use about a 6-inch (15 cm) square to get a card, 3x3-1/2-inch (7.5x9 cm) in size.

Suggested paper: From regular origami paper to decorative papers, like chiyogami, foil paper etc. Since the card displays two sides of paper, it is better to use duo-color paper.

Suggested color: Any you like. The brighter contrast between two sides of paper will be, the better.

If using two-color paper, begin with that side up, which color you would like to have on the heart.

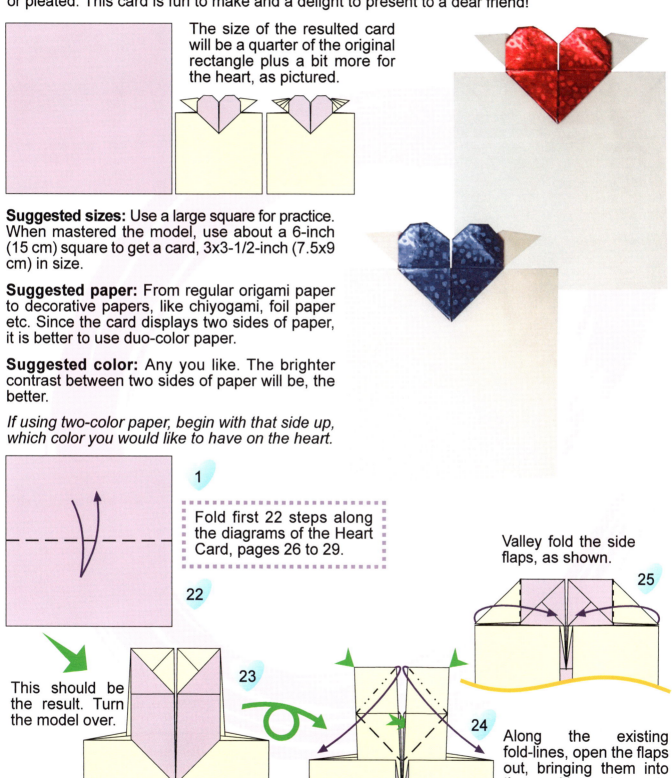

1

Fold first 22 steps along the diagrams of the Heart Card, pages 26 to 29.

22

This should be the result. Turn the model over.

23

24

Along the existing fold-lines, open the flaps out, bringing them into the position, shown in the next step.

Valley fold the side flaps, as shown.

25

Flying Heart Card © 2009 Katrin and Yuri Shumakov

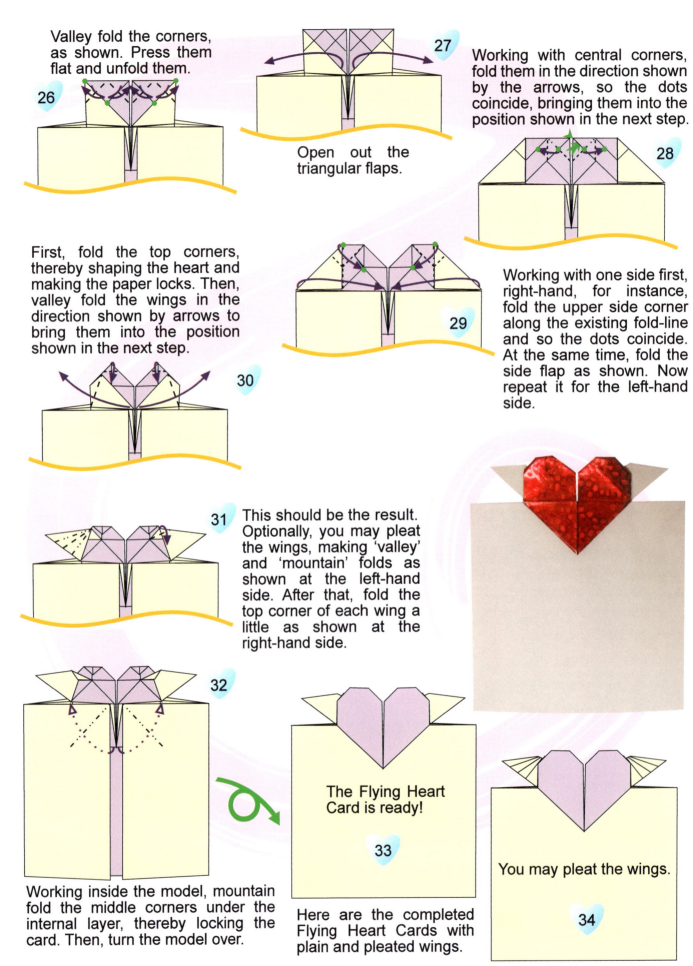

Flying Heart Card © 2009 Katrin and Yuri Shumakov

Flying Two-Heart Card
by Katrin and Yuri Shumakov

This card combines the folding techniques of the previous card designs with a result that's double lovely! It features two hearts - one is the body of the card itself and the other heart with wings on its top edge. This card is super cute and will be a great gift to a dear friend!

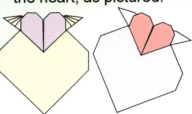

The size of the resulted card will be a quarter of the original rectangle plus a bit more for the heart, as pictured.

Suggested sizes: Use a large square for practice. When mastered the model, use about a 6-inch (15 cm) square to get a card, 3x3-1/2-inch (7.5x9 cm) in size.

Suggested paper: From regular origami paper to decorative papers, like chiyogami, foil paper etc. Since the card displays two sides of paper, it is better to use duo-color paper.

Suggested color: Any you like. The brighter contrast between two sides of paper will be, the better.

If using two-color paper, begin with that side up, which color you would like to have on the heart.

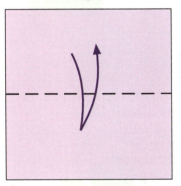

 1

First 31 steps are the same as for the Flying Heart Card, see pages 33 and 34.

 31

Continue folding along the steps 28 to 35 of the Two-Heart Card, pages 31 and 32.

28 35

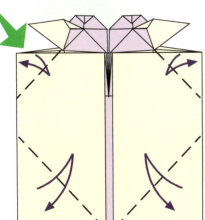

Here are the completed Flying Two-Heart Cards with plain and pleated wings.

Flying Two-Heart Card © 2009 Katrin and Yuri Shumakov

Double Heart
by Katrin Shumakov

This cute design folds from a square and features an identical heart on each side. The double heart can be used on its own or, due to the layers, it can be placed onto an edge of something, say, on a page of a book like a bookmark etc. This design also can be useful for making various decorations.

The finished model will be about 1/4 of the size of the original square, as pictured.

Suggested sizes: Use about a 4-inch (10 cm) square to get a 2-inch wide heart.

Suggested paper: From regular origami paper to decorative papers, like chiyogami, foil paper etc.

Suggested color: Any you like, though red and pink shades will work the best for hearts.

If using two-color paper, begin with colored side up.

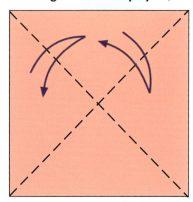

1 Valley fold the opposite corners together, in turn, to mark the diagonal fold-lines, and open them up. Turn the paper over.

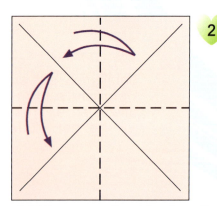

2 Valley fold the opposite sides together in both directions, and open them up.

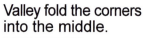

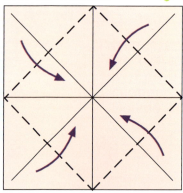

3 Valley fold the corners into the middle.

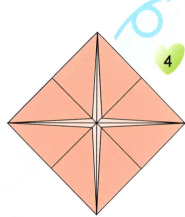

4 This should be the result. Turn the model over.

Double Heart © 1996 Katrin Shumakov

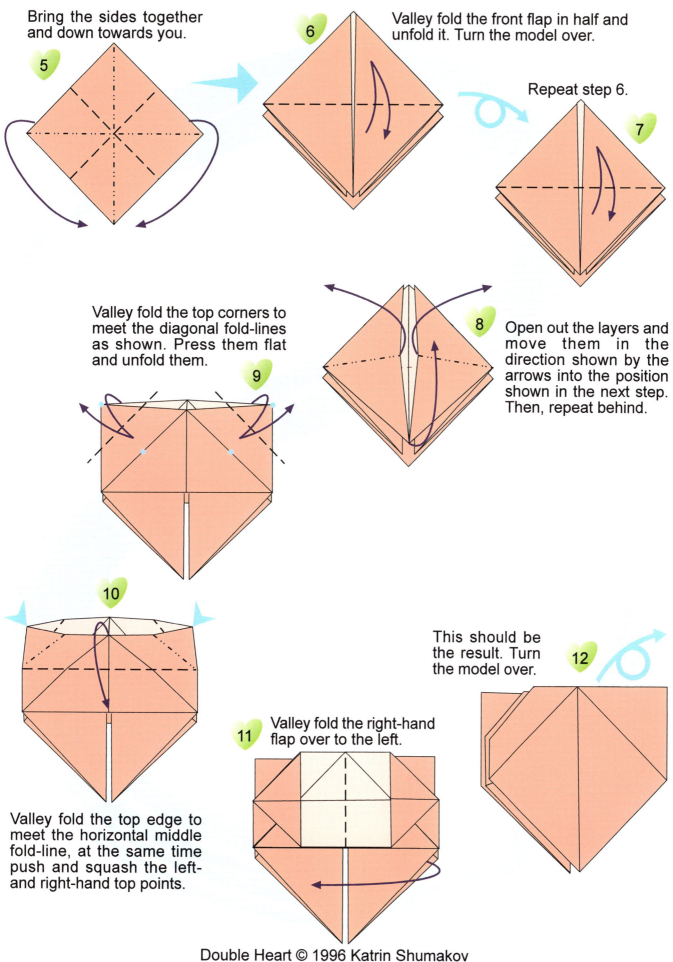

Double Heart © 1996 Katrin Shumakov

Origami Romantic Hearts

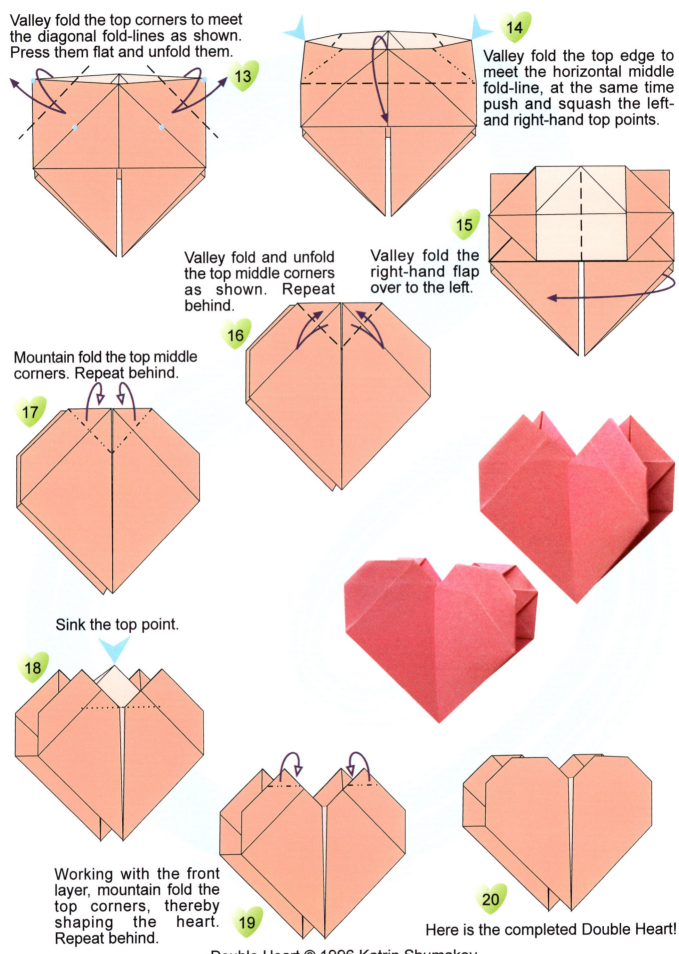

Double Heart © 1996 Katrin Shumakov

38   Origami Romantic Hearts

Double Heart Garland
by Katrin Shumakov

You can make a lovely hanging decoration with the double hearts. It could be one double heart tied with a ribbon or a whole garland of double hearts.

Take a piece of string or ribbon of an appropriate length. Fold in half and make a knot with the loop.

Fold the Double Heart as shown on pages 36 to 38.

1

Place the string ends between the layers of the double heart, enveloping the heart's core. Knot the two ends together and tie a bow, if you like.

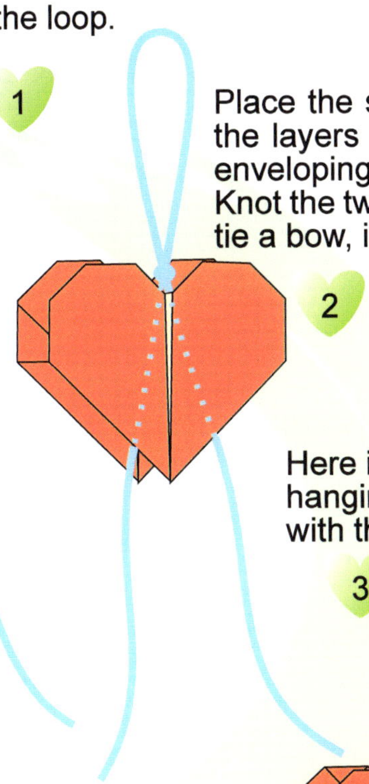

2

Here is the completed hanging decoration with the double heart.

3

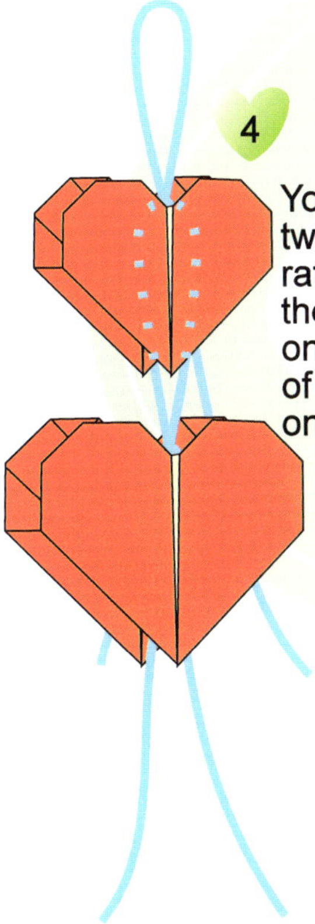

4

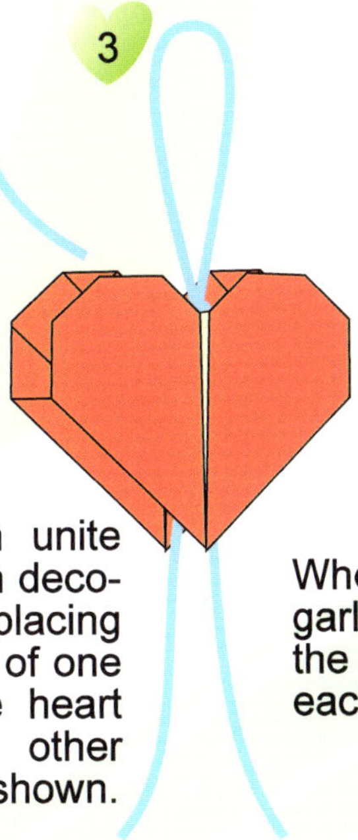

You can unite two such decorations, placing the loop of one onto the heart of the other one, as shown.

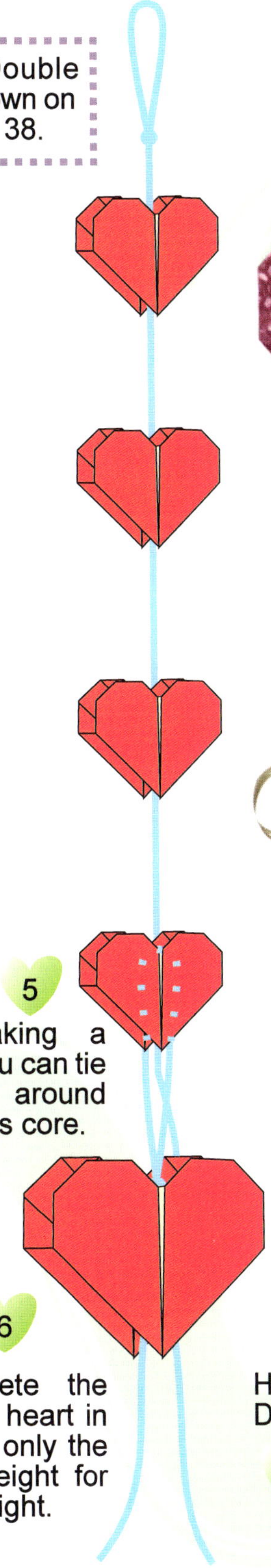

5

When making a garland, you can tie the string around each heart's core.

6

You can also complete the garland with the bigger heart in the end - it will add not only the charm, but also the weight for the garland to hang straight.

Here is the completed Double Heart Garland.

7

Double Heart Garland © 1996 Katrin Shumakov

Double Heart Card
by Katrin Shumakov

Due to its design, the double heart is perfect for making a romantic card that opens like a cupboard with two doors. You can make a symmetrical cupboard fold card or an asymmetrical one.

Suggested sizes: Use regular sized card stock, 1/2 of Letter or A4. For the hearts, use about 4-inch to 2-inch (10 to 5 cm) squares, depending on your idea for a card.

Suggested paper: For the card itself, use card stock. For the heart, use regular origami paper or any decorative papers.

Suggested color: Any you like, red and pink shades will work the best for hearts.

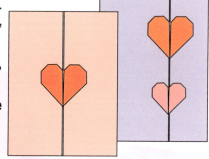

Fold the Double Hearts as shown on pages 36 to 38.

1. Mark the fold-lines out on your card to get the cupboard-like form with two doors that can be opened and closed. You can do doors symmetrical or asymmetrical, as in this case.

2. Define the place for each of the double hearts. Then glue them to the opposite edges, so the layers of the one half of the heart are enveloping the edge and glued to it by the heart's core.

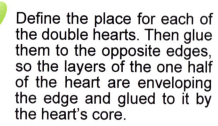

3. Close the flaps of your card at the same time inserting the card's edges into the slots of the opposite hearts.

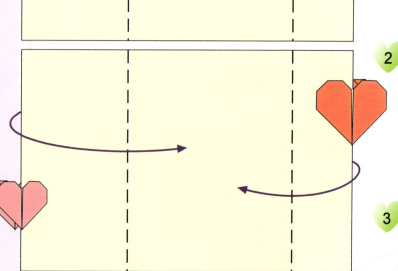

4. Here is the completed asymmetrical cupboard-like card with the Double Hearts.

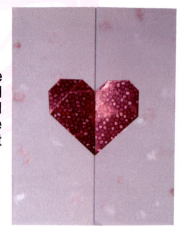

5. Here is the completed symmetrical cupboard-like Double Heart Card.

Double Heart Card © 1996 Katrin Shumakov

Flying Heart
by Yuri Shumakov

This lovely design folds from a square and features wings on the heart. The flying heart makes a wonderful valentine on its own and can be used to decorate cards.

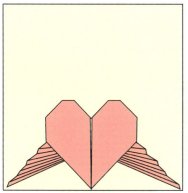

The finished model will be about 1/2 of the size of the original square, as pictured.

Suggested sizes: Use about a 4-inch (10 cm) square to get a 2-inch wide heart with a 4-inch wingspan.

Suggested paper: From regular origami paper to decorative papers, like chiyogami, foil paper etc.

Suggested color: Any you like.

If using two-color paper, begin with colored side down.

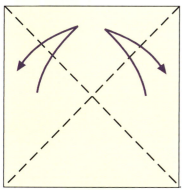

1

Valley fold the opposite corners together, in turn, to mark the diagonal fold lines, and open them up.

Valley fold the upper right- and left-hand corners to meet the intersection of the fold-lines made in step 1. Press them flat.

2

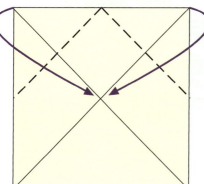

3

Mountain fold the top triangle back along its bottom border.

Valley fold the top corners along the existing fold-lines.

4

Flying Heart © 1998 Yuri Shumakov

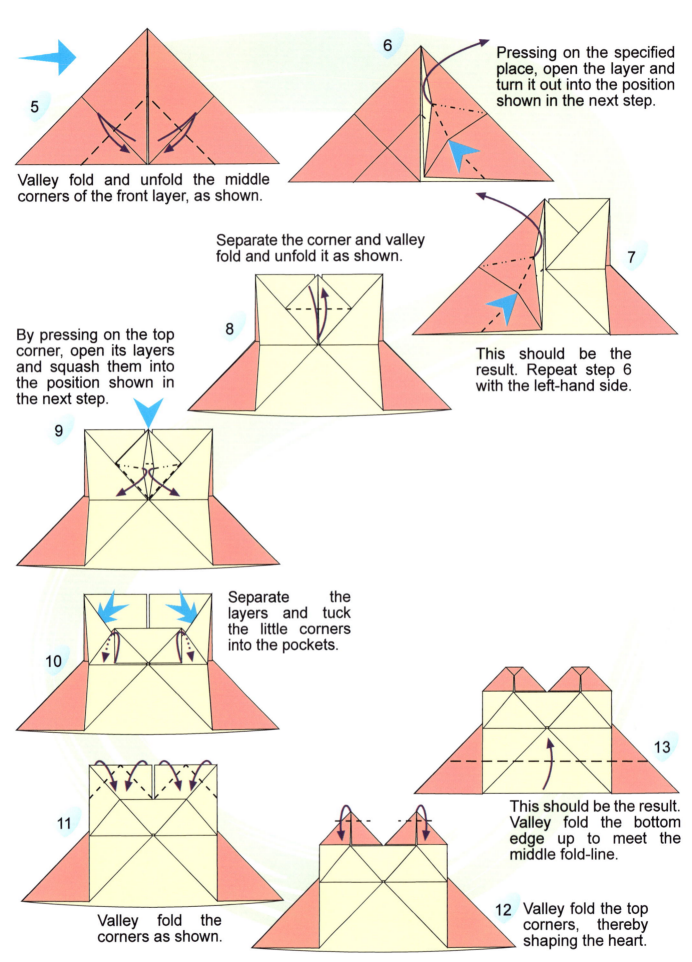

Flying Heart © 1998 Yuri Shumakov

Origami Romantic Hearts

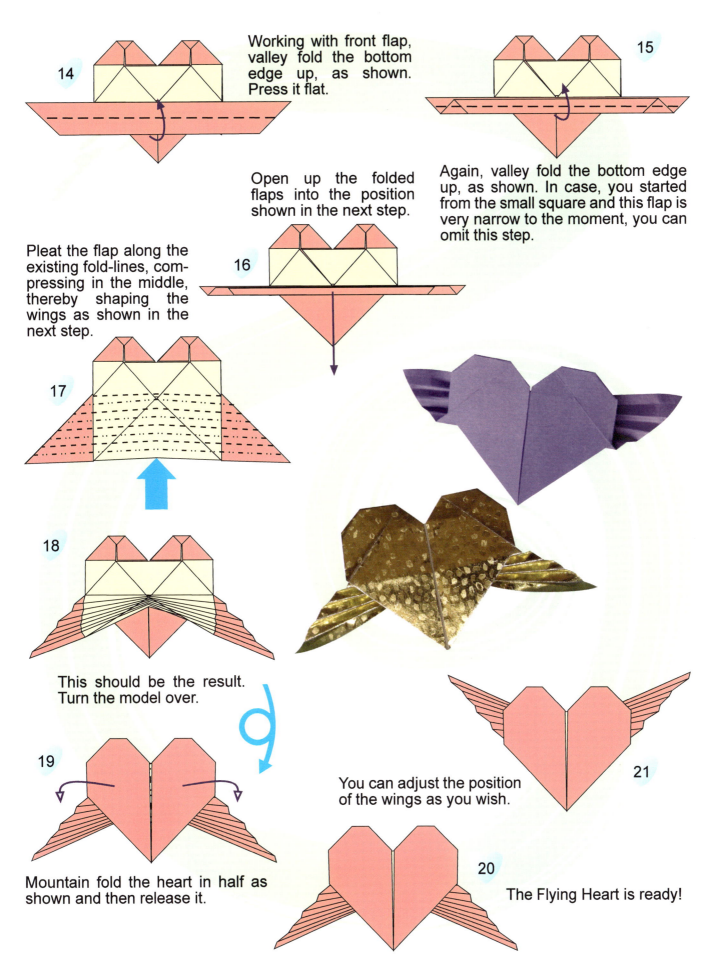

Valentine
by Yuri Shumakov

This is a lovely design of a free standing card with the heart on its top edge. It may be folded down flat to be inserted into an envelope, for instance. It is fun to fold and will be perfect for Valentine's Day as well as for any other romantic occasion.

The card folds from a rectangle of paper, approximately 4:1 in proportion. The size of the resulted card will be a bit less of the half of the original rectangle, as pictured.

The width of the card will be the same as the width of the original rectangle. The top square will used to shape the heart and the 'shoulders' of the card, the rest of paper will be used to form the standing card itself.

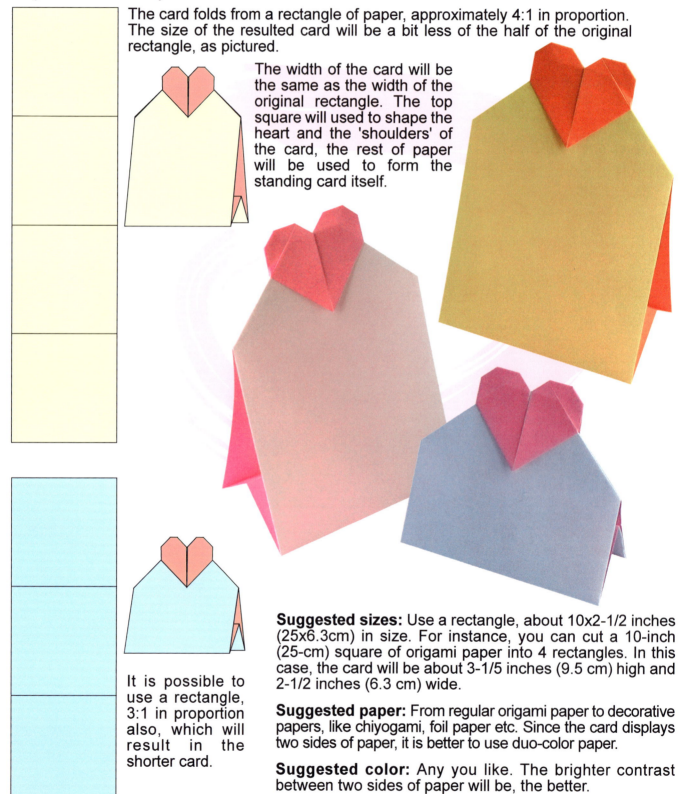

It is possible to use a rectangle, 3:1 in proportion also, which will result in the shorter card.

Suggested sizes: Use a rectangle, about 10x2-1/2 inches (25x6.3cm) in size. For instance, you can cut a 10-inch (25-cm) square of origami paper into 4 rectangles. In this case, the card will be about 3-1/5 inches (9.5 cm) high and 2-1/2 inches (6.3 cm) wide.

Suggested paper: From regular origami paper to decorative papers, like chiyogami, foil paper etc. Since the card displays two sides of paper, it is better to use duo-color paper.

Suggested color: Any you like. The brighter contrast between two sides of paper will be, the better.

Valentine © 1998 Yuri Shumakov

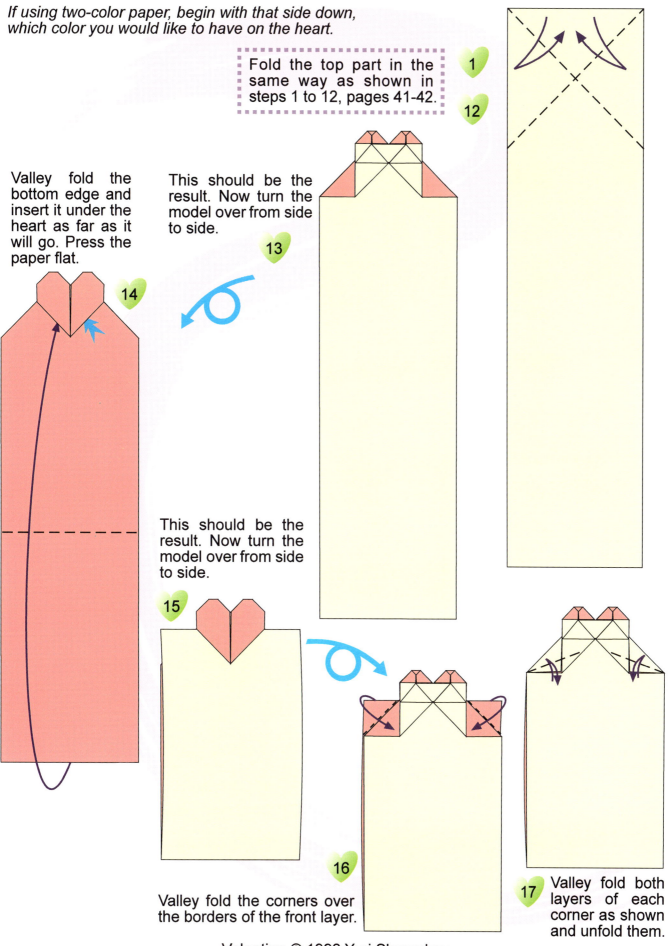

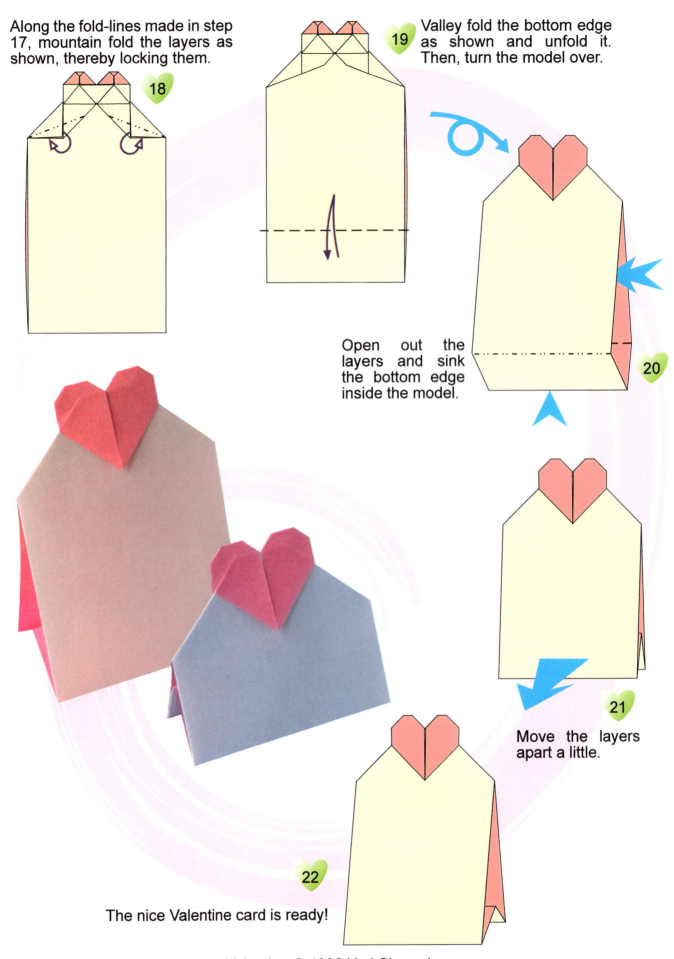

Heart Rings
by Yuri Shumakov

This lovely ring design comes in two variations - One-Color Heart Ring and Two-Color Heart Ring. Each folds from a strip of paper, 1:8 in proportion or so, and is fun to make. The heart ring will do a perfect gift to your loved one! Also when folded from a large strip, this design will make a romantic napkin ring!

The height of the heart gem of the finished ring will be the same as the height of the original rectangle, as pictured.

Suggested sizes: For practice, take a large strip, say, 1x8 inches (2.5x20 cm) in size or bigger. When mastered the model, use a strip, about 3/4x6 inches (2x16 cm) in size to get a ring suitable for a finger.

Suggested paper: From regular origami paper to decorative papers. Foil paper will work especially well. For the two-color ring, it is better to use duo-color paper.

Suggested color: Any you like.

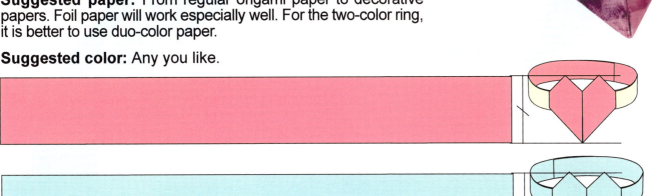

Two-Color Heart Ring

If using two-color paper, begin with that side up, which color you would like to have on the heart.

 Valley fold the strip in half from right to left.

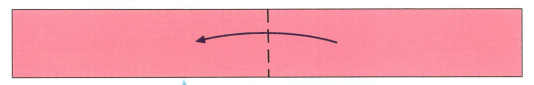

Separate the front layer and valley fold its bottom edge over to lie along the right-hand side. Do not press the paper completely flat, but just press down on its top a little. Unfold it.

Valley fold the right-hand side over the intersection of the top edge and the fold-mark made in step 2. Press the paper flat and unfold it.

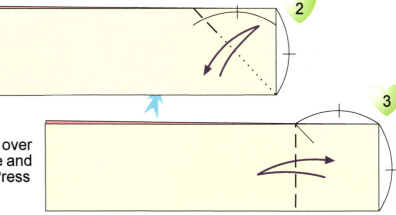

Heart Rings © 2001 Yuri Shumakov

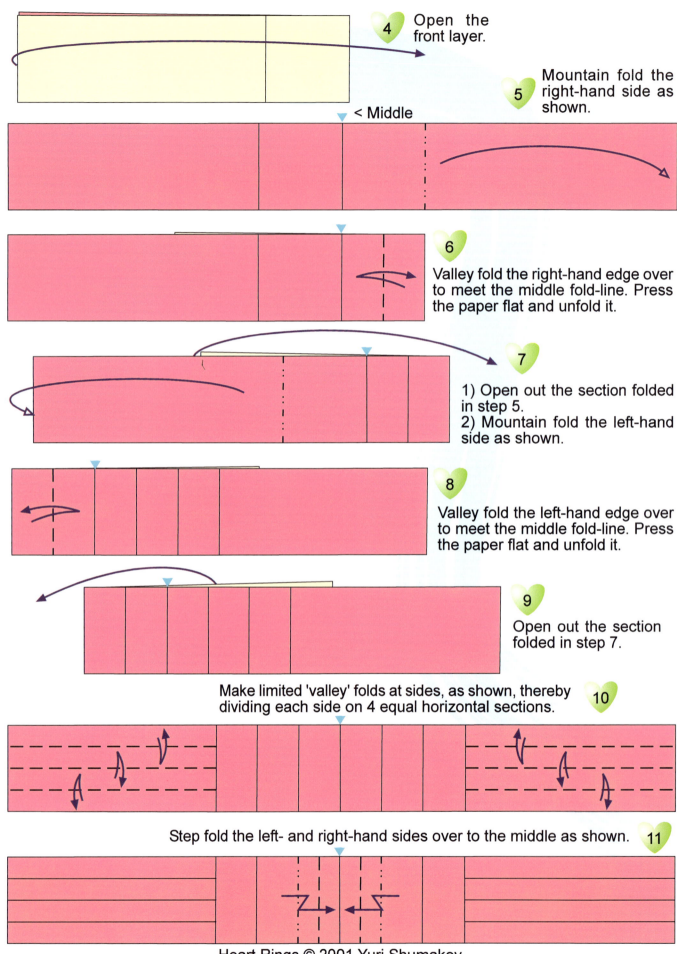

Heart Rings © 2001 Yuri Shumakov

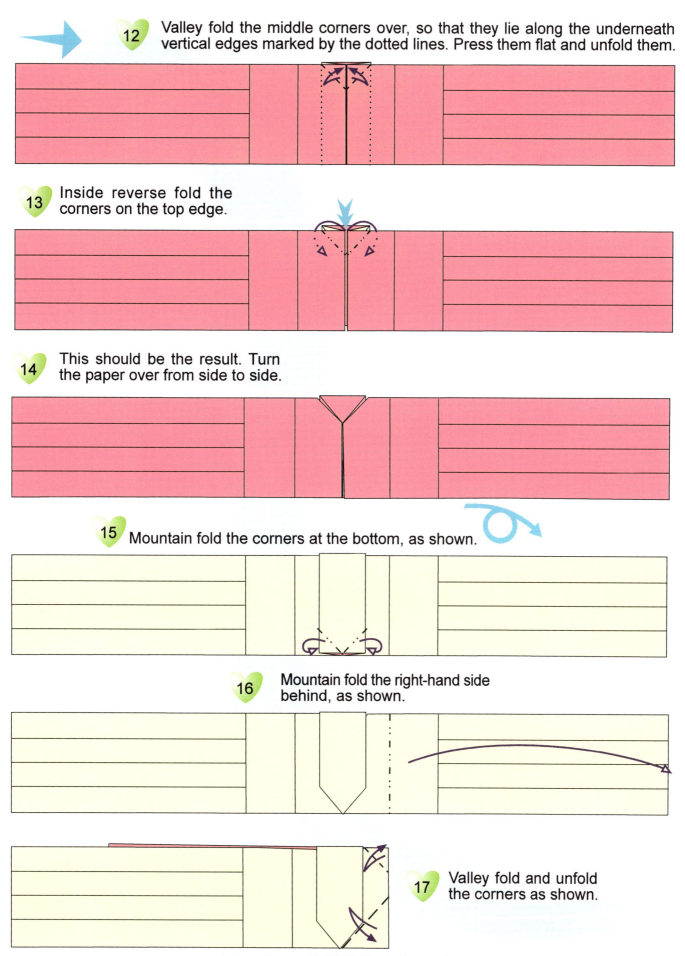

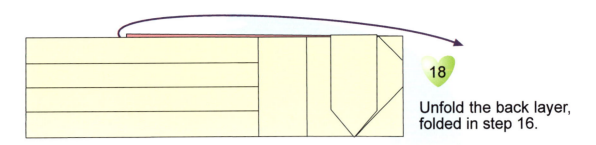

18 Unfold the back layer, folded in step 16.

19 Mountain fold the left-hand side behind, as shown. Then, as in mirror, repeat steps 17 and 18 for the left-hand side.

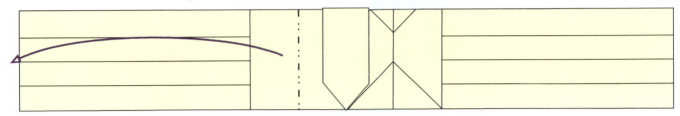

20 Along existing fold-lines, fold the right-hand side over to the left, at the same time shaping the paper into the position shown in the next step.

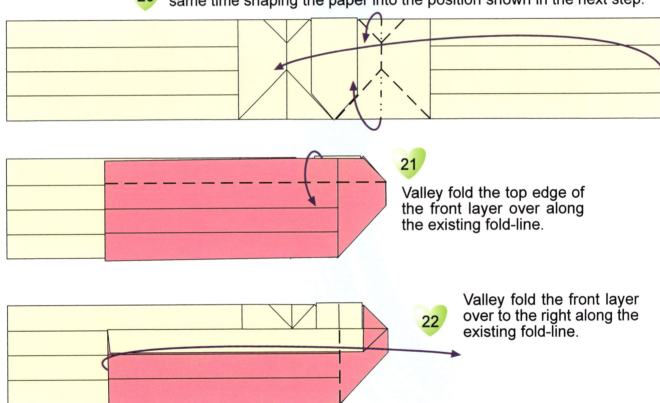

21 Valley fold the top edge of the front layer over along the existing fold-line.

22 Valley fold the front layer over to the right along the existing fold-line.

As in mirror, repeat steps 20-22 for the left-hand side.

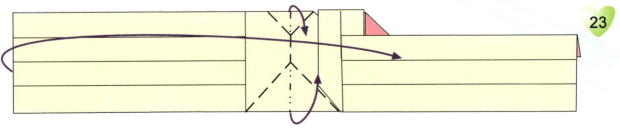

23

Heart Rings © 2001 Yuri Shumakov

50   Origami Romantic Hearts

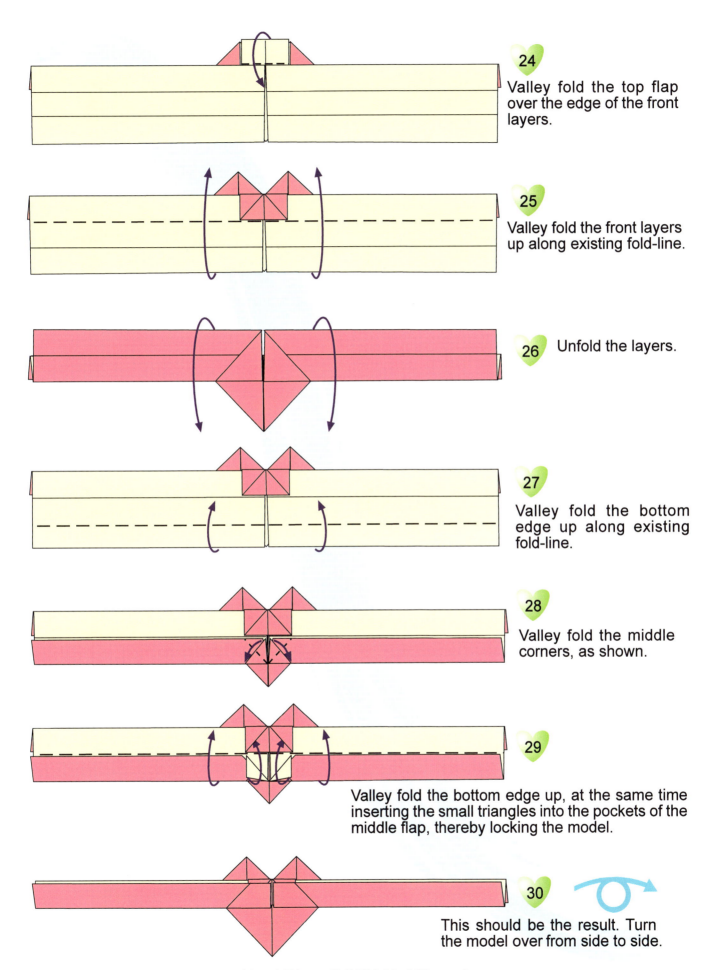

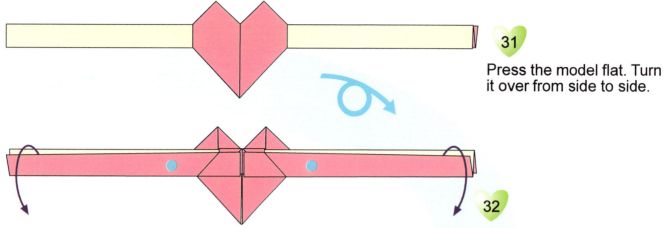

31. Press the model flat. Turn it over from side to side.

32. Open the layers on the right- and left-hand sides into the position shown in the next step. Keep the middle part locked; if on some reason it opens - do not worry, you can lock it again when competing the ring in step 34.

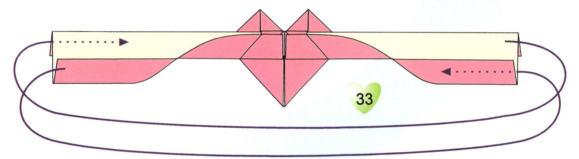

33. Carefully insert the one end inside the other as far as needed for the appropriate size of the ring.

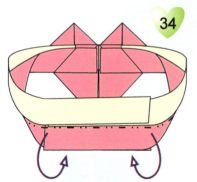

34. Mountain fold the bottom edge inside, thereby completing the ring. Check the lock on the 'heart' part and if it opened, fix it.

35. This should be the result. Turn the ring around.

Here is the finished Two-Color Ring with the heart gem.

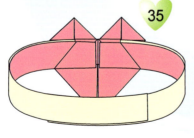

Heart Rings © 2001 Yuri Shumakov

One-Color Heart Ring

1 – 20 Fold the first 20 steps in the same way as shown for the first variation of the heart ring, pages 47-50.

21 Valley fold the front flap over to the right along the existing fold-line.

22 Valley fold the top edge of the right-hand side along the existing fold-line, as shown.

23 This should be the result. Along existing fold-lines, fold the left-hand side over to the right. Then, as in mirror, repeat steps 21-22 for the left-hand side.

24 This should be the result. Valley fold the top flap over the edge of the front layers.

25 – 35 Fold steps 25 to 35 in the same way as shown on pages 51 to 52.

36 Here is the completed One-Color Heart Ring.

Heart Rings © 2001 Yuri Shumakov

Origami Romantic Hearts

Heart Bracelet
by Yuri Shumakov

This lovely modular bracelet will be a wonderful addition to the origami heart ring! In fact, the module of the bracelet is based on the heart ring design, so they are quite related. The several modules are connected into a bracelet with only paper locks, no glue. Of course, it's possible to make this bracelet from one long strip, but with modules it's much easier and fun, besides you can mix colors.

The height (as well as the width) of the heart gem of the bracelet will be the same as the height of the original rectangle used for a module, as pictured.

Suggested sizes: For each module, use a rectangle of paper, 1:5 in proportion, for instance, 1x5 inches (2.5x10 cm) in size. You will need approximately 8 modules or so, depending on the needed size. In this case, the circumference of the 8-module bracelet will be 8 inches (20 cm).

Suggested paper: From regular origami paper to decorative papers. Foil paper will work especially well.

Suggested color: Any you like.

Heart Module (Two-Color or One-Color)

The heart module folds in the same way as the heart ring, only from a rectangle, 1:5 in proportion. You may choose to make Two-Color Heart Modules or One-Color Heart Modules. Visually there will be no significant difference between two versions of the heart bracelet. It's just the Two-Color version will have the second color appear between the heart gems.

Two-Color Heart Module — or — One-Color Heart Module

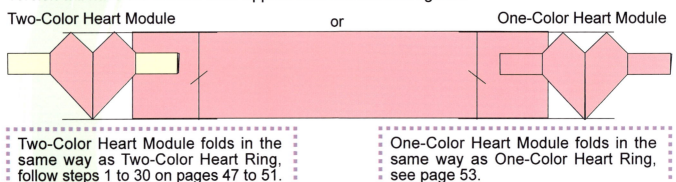

Two-Color Heart Module folds in the same way as Two-Color Heart Ring, follow steps 1 to 30 on pages 47 to 51.

One-Color Heart Module folds in the same way as One-Color Heart Ring, see page 53.

Bracelet Assembly (Two-Color Heart Modules)

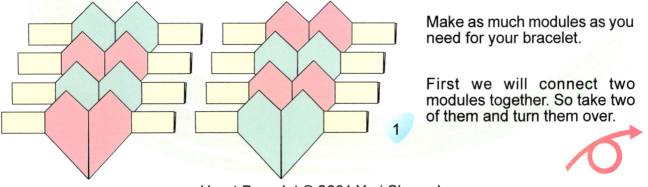

Make as much modules as you need for your bracelet.

First we will connect two modules together. So take two of them and turn them over.

Heart Bracelet © 2001 Yuri Shumakov

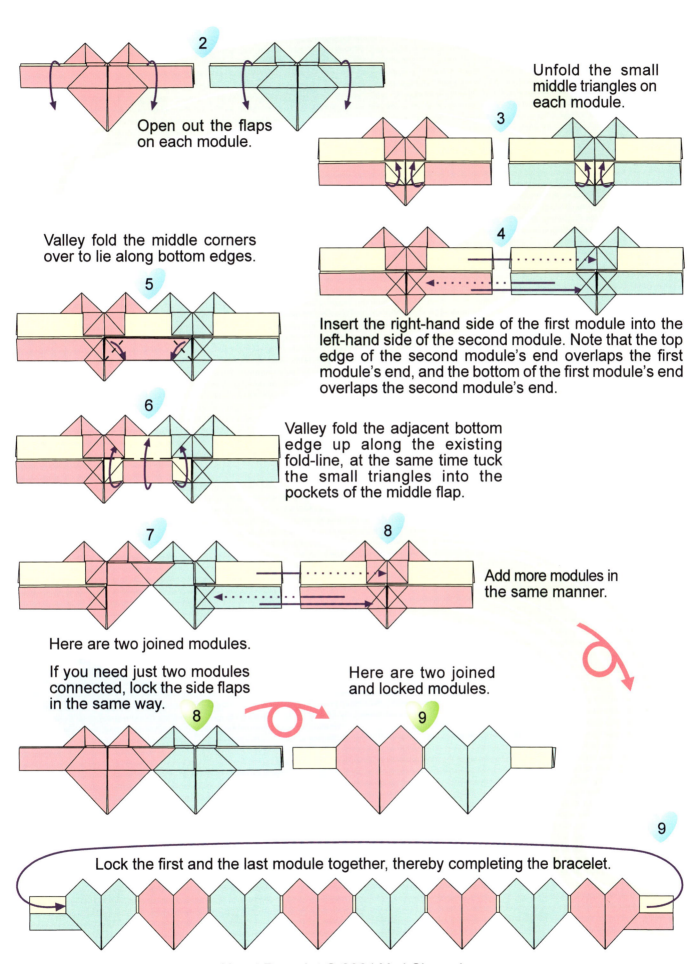

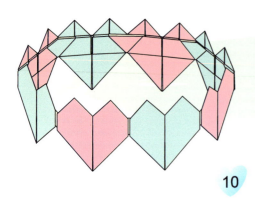

10

Here is the completed Heart Bracelet from two-color modules.

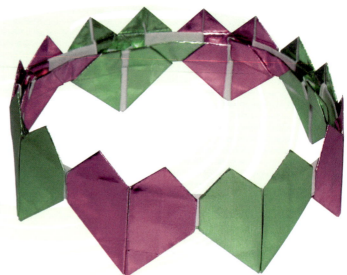

Bracelet Assembly (One-Color Heart Modules)

If you have chosen to make One-Color Heart Modules for your Heart Bracelet, there is a slight difference in the assembly process.

> The first 3 steps are the same as for the assembly of the first variation (see pages 54-55).

1
3

4

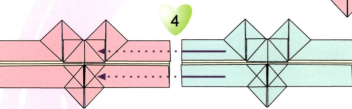

Insert the left-hand side of the second module into the right-hand side of the first module. Note that one end completely overlaps the other.

5 Valley fold the middle corners over to lie along bottom edges.

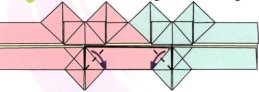

> Continue in the same manner as shown in steps 6 to 10 on pages 55-56.

6
10

Here is the completed Heart Bracelet from one-color modules.

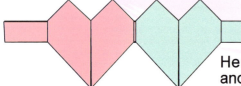

Here are two joined and locked modules.

Heart Bracelet © 2001 Yuri Shumakov

Heart Wristband
by Yuri Shumakov

This elegant wristband adds a perfect romantic touch to your outfit and will make a terrific gift to your special friend! In addition, when folded in an appropriate size it can be used as a cute headband!

The height (as well as the width) of the heart gem of the wristband will be the same as the height of the original rectangle, as pictured.

Suggested sizes: For the heart module, use a rectangle of paper, 1:5 in proportion, for instance, 1x5 inches (2.5x10 cm) in size. For the wristband, use a long strip of the same height and the needed length, for instance, 1x8 inches (2.5x20 cm) in size. In this case, the circumference of the wristband will be 8 inches (20 cm).

Suggested paper: From regular origami paper to decorative papers. Foil paper will work especially well.

Fold the Heart Module in the same way as Two-Color Heart Ring, follow steps 1 to 30 on pages 47 to 51.

Suggested color: Any you like.

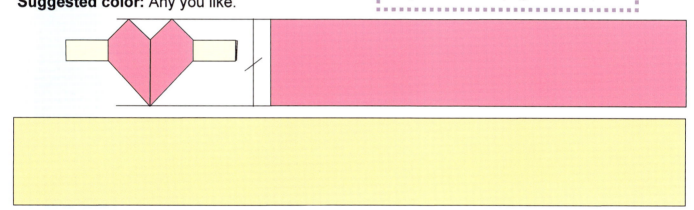

1 Turn the module on its back and open out the flaps.

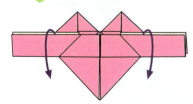
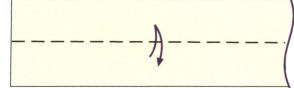

For the band strip, begin with colored side down. Valley fold the strip in half, press the paper flat and unfold it.

2 Unfold the small middle triangles of the heart module.

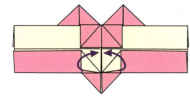
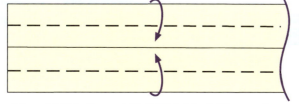

Valley fold the top and bottom edges of the strip over to meet the horizontal middle fold-line.

Heart Wristband © 2001 Yuri Shumakov

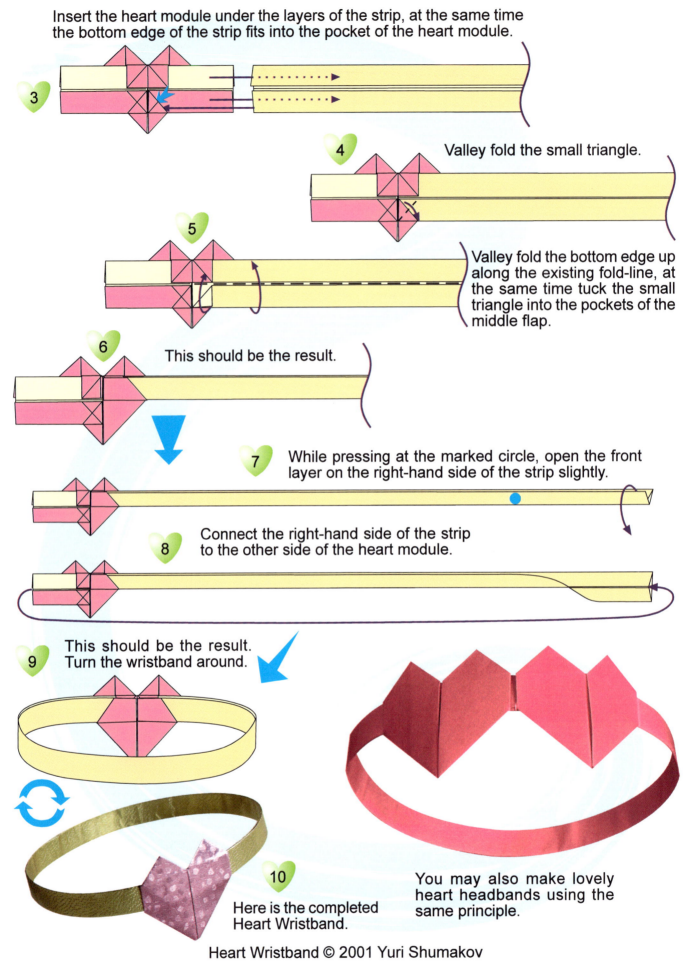

Heart Balloon
by Yuri Shumakov

This volumetric design will add much fun to your romantic time. The heart balloon folds from a square of paper. You also will need a strip, 1:4 in proportion, to make a thread / thin stick to keep the balloon on.

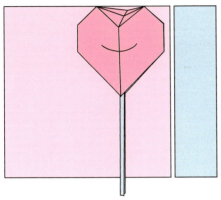

Suggested paper: Regular origami paper.

Suggested sizes: Use a 6-inch (15 cm) square and a strip 1-1/2x6 inches (3.75x15cm). Or a 5-inch (12.5 cm) square and a strip 1-1/4x5 inches (3x12.5cm).

Suggested colors: Red, pink or blue will do nicely.

The finished heart will be about a quarter of the initial square as pictured.

Begin with colored side down.

Valley fold the square in half from side to side. Press it flat and unfold it.

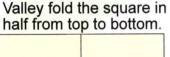

Valley fold the square in half from top to bottom.

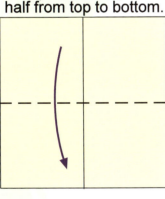

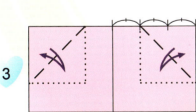

Valley fold the upper right-hand corner about 2/3 to the middle into the position shown by the dotted line. Press the fold flat and unfold it. Repeat for the left-hand side.

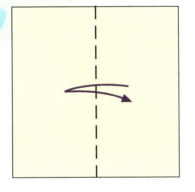

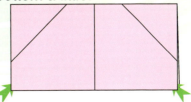

This should be the result. Open the model out from the bottom a little.

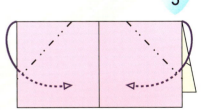

Along the fold-lines made in step 3, inside reverse fold the side corners into the model.

Heart Balloon © 2014 Yuri Shumakov

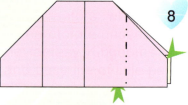

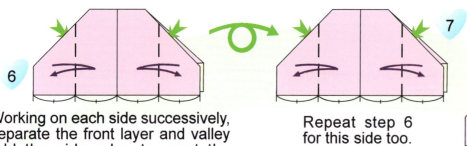

6 Working on each side successively, separate the front layer and valley fold the side edge to meet the vertical middle line. Press it flat and unfold it. Then, turn the model over from side to side.

7 Repeat step 6 for this side too.

8 Working with the front layer, open it a little bit and along the existing fold-lines, inside reverse fold the side point into the model.

9 In the process.

10 Repeat steps 8-9 with left-hand side, thereby inside reverse fold the side point into the model.

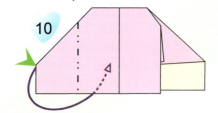

11 This should be the result. Now turn the model over from side to side.

12 Repeat steps 8-10 for this side too.

13 This should be the result.

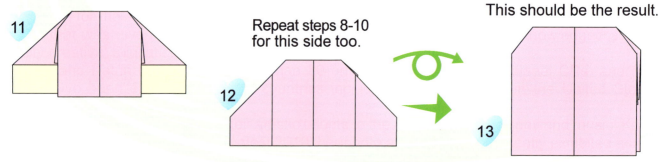

The following steps are shown as the photo-diagrams.

14 Take the model and turn it around into the position shown in the next step.

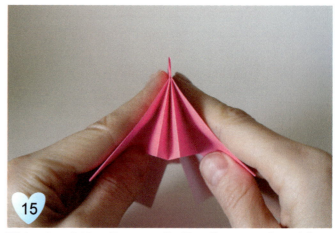

15 This should be the result. Gently open the sides, so that the upper part remains compressed.

Heart Balloon © 2014 Yuri Shumakov

16

Turn the model toward you. Working with the upper part, gently push the left-hand side of the open folds, so that the layers coincide as shown in the next step.

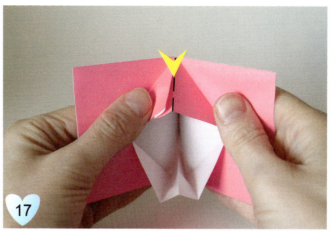

17

This should be the result. Now push the layers into the model, re-forming the vertical middle line into a 'valley'.

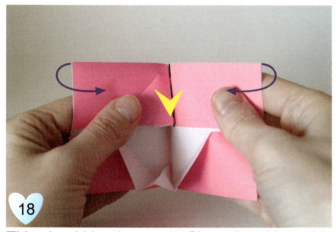

18

This should be the result. Close the sides a bit, so that the layers are alighted inside.

19

Now turn the model around and repeat steps 16-18 for the other open folds.

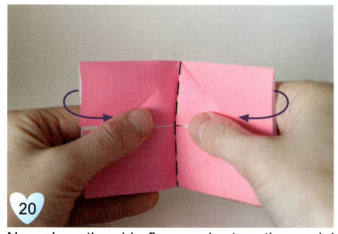

20

Now close the side flaps and return the model into the initial position.

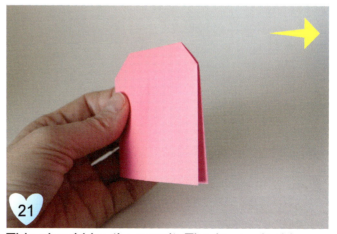

21

This should be the result. The layers inside are locked.
The following steps are shown in the vector diagrams.

Heart Balloon © 2014 Yuri Shumakov

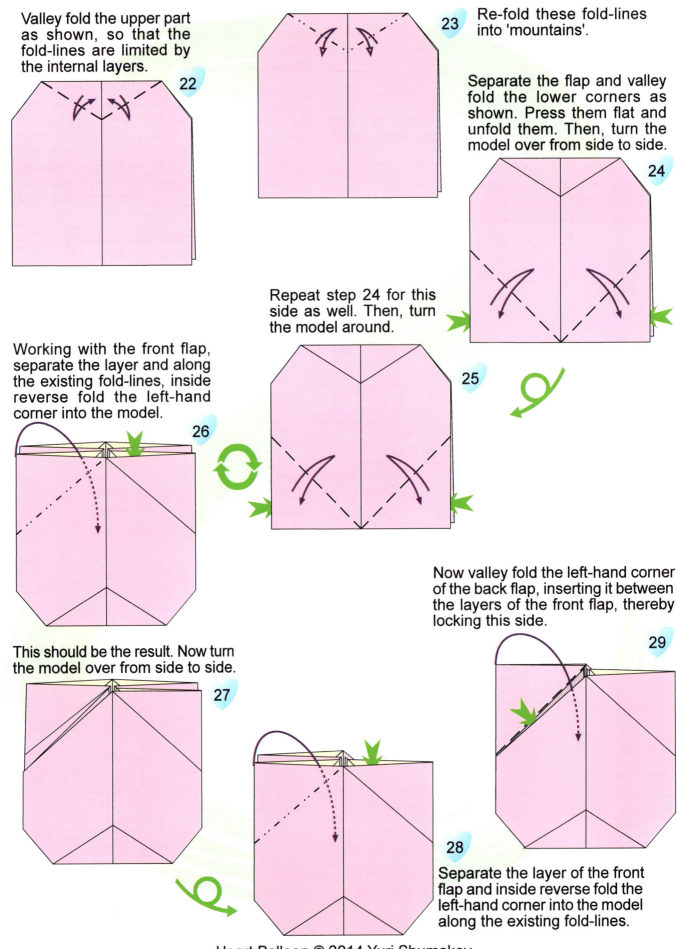

Heart Balloon © 2014 Yuri Shumakov

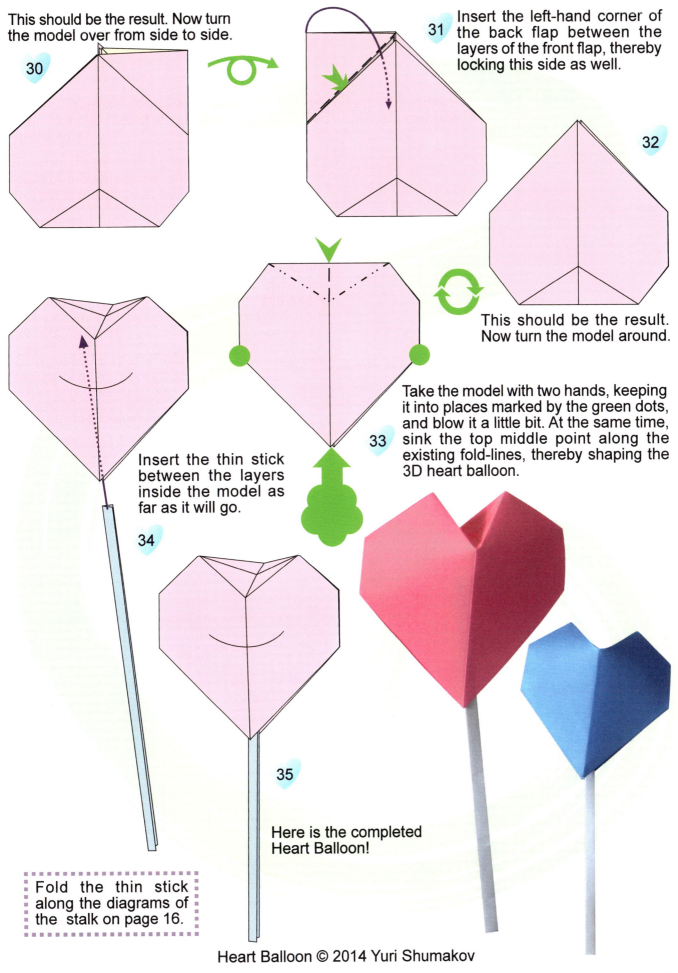

About Authors

Yuri and Katrin Shumakov - a stellar artist-duo, professional origami creators, who started their origami journey in France in 1989 and since then unfold this art in a heretofore unseen way!

They have created amazing paper world ORILAND with incredible fantasy Kingdoms that impress with rich detail of majestic castles, abundance of paper flora and busy life of little paper dwellers. Their newest kingdoms Toy-ronto and Albuquerque combine fantasy and reality together, presenting a whimsical artistic rendition of iconic sights of these cities.

Another beautiful and elegant aspect of origami they brought to life is ORIBANA - a marriage of two Japanese arts: Origami and Ikebana. By combining these remarkable art-forms, in early 1990s Katrin and Yuri began to create paper flower arrangements in paper vases and thought up a distinctive name for it - Oribana. Since then they designed more than 50 charming oribana-compositions with a broad variety of origami flowers, leaves and vases.

Being prolific origami authors they created more than a thousand of origami designs from simple forms and cute characters to complex dinosaurs' skeletons and architecture that all have a distinctive Oriland style. Their Oriland Magic Star is a big action origami hit that amazes and dazzles with its mesmerizing effect when rotated.

Psychologists by education, Katrin and Yuri Shumakov have studied how origami helps children learn. Their Ph.D scientific work shows that by doing origami, children develop better use of both hands, whether they are left- or right- handed. They also discovered that origami can improve creativity and intelligence in children ages 7 to 11. They believe that origami is "entertainment for the soul, gymnastics for the mind, and training for the hands."

In 1999, Yuri and Katrin received the Silver Award in the ThinkQuest International Competition for their 'Travel to Oriland' website and it brought them and their team to Universal Studios Hollywood for the Award Ceremony! Their Oriland.com website became a winner of the Childnet Award that was given them in Paris, France. Both these projects were acknowledged as high quality creative, educational and fun websites for children and adults.

Yuri and Katrin have written more than 30 origami books and instructional CDs, and their works have been exhibited in many countries including several venues in the United States, France, Spain and Canada.

The Shumakovs also extend their artistic talents to the realm of photography and music. Katrin is a winner of the Toronto Photo Contest 2010; her photo art-works were recently exhibited across Canada. Yuri is enjoying music composing and sound design; he has released eight music albums in Space, Ambient, New Age and Smooth Jazz genres.

Katrin and Yuri live in Toronto, Canada, love yoga and a healthy style of life.

Visit their Oriland website to see what origami can be!

http://www.oriland.com

Oriland's TOY-RONTO Kingdom, Canadian National Exhibition, Toronto, ON, Canada, 2013.

CPSIA information can be obtained
at www.ICGtesting.com
Printed in the USA
LVIC04n0927161015
458555LV00002B/4